A Brief History of
the Future of Education

A Brief History of
the Future of Education

Learning in the Age of Disruption

Ian Jukes

Ryan L. Schaaf

Foreword by Steve Wozniak

CORWIN

A SAGE Publishing Company

FOR INFORMATION:

Corwin

A SAGE Company

2455 Teller Road

Thousand Oaks, California 91320

(800) 233-9936

www.corwin.com

SAGE Publications Ltd.

1 Oliver's Yard

55 City Road

London EC1Y 1SP

United Kingdom

SAGE Publications India Pvt. Ltd.

B 1/I 1 Mohan Cooperative Industrial Area

Mathura Road, New Delhi 110 044

India

SAGE Publications Asia-Pacific Pte. Ltd.

18 Cross Street #10-10/11/12

China Square Central

Singapore 048423

Printed in the United States of America

ISBN 978-1-5443-5502-3

This book is printed on acid-free paper.

SFI label applies to text stock

Publisher: Arnis Burvikovs

Development Editor: Desirée A. Bartlett

Editorial Assistant: Eliza Erickson

Production Editor: Amy Schroller

Copy Editor: Liann Lech

Typesetter: C&M Digitals (P) Ltd.

Proofreader: Dennis W. Webb

Indexer: Amy Murphy

Cover Designer: Scott Van Atta

Marketing Manager: Sharon Pendergast

19 20 21 22 23 10 9 8 7 6 5 4 3 2 1

CONTENTS

FOREWORD

There's today, and then there's the future.

We grow up with assumptions about how the modern world works. We live in and adapt to the guides and resources we hope will lead us to jobs and money and homes and families and happiness. We are surrounded by clues about how life works and hints of what we need to do to achieve our desired results. Life ahead appears very promising.

And then, just like that, things change—quickly—and a lot! Change in our families; change in our communities; change in our world!

It's easy to say that we have to adapt, but it's harder to actually change. The changes in our lifetime are the result of the emergence of the new digital landscape. Inexpensive and powerful digital tools have fundamentally transformed the way we work and the way we play in the world in which we live. I look at all the activities I do on a daily basis with my digital tools and wonder how I ever did without them.

Let's consider just a few of these dynamic changes. Using today's digital tools and the Internet, we can now manage our online accounts without ever stepping into a bank. We can shop without ever leaving the comfort of our home. A person with a smartphone and the necessary research skills can easily be the smartest person in the room. We can travel to far off places without ever flying in a plane, boarding a train, or going on a road trip. We can develop friendships with countless people who we might never meet in person. We can spend hours of our time watching funny and creative videos on YouTube; as well as effortlessly producing our own multimedia creations. The possibilities are endless. We can do things today that would have seemed unimaginable even a decade ago. And because this all seems to have happened so quickly, it can feel absolutely overwhelming. It's certainly true for me.

And these dramatic changes and their implications for our futures can seem insurmountable. Newspapers have been replaced by websites and social media feeds. CDs and MP3 players have been replaced by anytime, anywhere streamed music. DVDs used to provide much of our video entertainment, yet they have quickly been dethroned by Netflix. Paper books are rapidly being replaced by e-readers and iBooks. Many of us are in denial even as this continues to happen right before our very eyes. It's like a huge bulldozer knocking down our long-standing perspectives.

Because we are human, we fight the inevitable and visible changes at both the unconscious and conscious levels. We have deeply embedded memories of how things were when we were growing up. Take schools for example. Even though an everyday, taken-for-granted tool in our lives is access to digital devices connected to the internet, we continue to structure schools the way it has always been organized—the same organizational structures, roles, emphasis on content, and schedules that have traditionally been used. The challenge of change is that taking a traditional approach increasingly doesn't work. That's why it's time to rethink schools. It's time to rethink learning. It's time to use modern tools and thinking to cultivate next generation learning skills that will help transform existing educational paradigms.

When my children were young, I discovered they were far more attracted to educationally oriented programs that resembled real people. Every time the graphics got more realistic, and the voices sounded less like C3PO and more like Mr. Rogers, the more they were attracted to their devices. It was as if they were friends. They learned from their devices and software because the tools and the media catered to their interests—customized and personalized for their individual consumption. While we've made incredible progress, we still have a great distance to go to make the tools indistinguishable from humans.

The future of our nation is in the hands of today's learners. It's in the values, social methodologies, and ways of arriving at solutions that define the world as we know it. Yet, for any number of reasons, education seems to be struggling coming to terms with the new digital world. Even many young teachers today struggle because, as students and student teachers, they were brought up in the traditional educational system. As a result, students often unconsciously revert to the expectations, experiences, and assumptions of their teachers, and don't develop the modern mindsets increasingly necessary for the new digital landscape.

I look at students today and marvel at how intuitively they use digital tools in their everyday lives outside of school. Then, I think of the possibilities for a class of 30 young students. Today, as it has long been, a presentation from a teacher is typically fixed for all of the learners in a class. They all get the same presentation of material. Then, a test is used to provide a variable grade that sorts the students out primarily on their ability to memorize. If a student happens to be on the low-end during their early years, they frequently don't value their education and often come to assume that they can never compete with others who are good at memorizing things.

Now, imagine the same scenario with 30 digital devices acting as 30 personalized teachers. Imagine a learning environment that permits every student to progress at a different rate for different subjects. Imagine a learning environment shaped by personal interests and abilities. Imagine a learning environment designed to enhance competency for every student until they have mastered all of the essential skills and content for each subject area. If learners decide to earn straight As, this is an environment that can assist them in their goals. If learners want to go deeper into a particular subject, this environment can empower them. In traditional learning, when time is the constant, learning becomes the variable. When device-supported learning becomes the constant, time becomes the variable. Creating these types of learning environments has the potential to overcome the traditional paradigms of schools. The big challenge is not the potential of digital tools to accomplish this, but rather overcoming the traditional mindsets that become the obstacle to allowing this to happen.

Many people talk about the need to teach thinking rather than memorization. The challenge is that, in many schools, we learn very early not to question ideas too deeply. We don't open up cabinets to satisfy our curiosity about what's inside. We don't spend time on topics that we find interesting. Rather, there's specific curriculum that must be covered. And we learn continually that there is only one right answer—an answer that is the same for everyone. It's usually a negative factor to ask why something is so. We learn to calculate when two trains will meet on the tracks—something we'll never need in life, but very few students ever raise their hands to ask why they are learning this, or what possible connection this has to their everyday lives.

Also, I worry most about turning off the creative instincts that our children are born with, by not letting them follow their passions and hearts. Traditional learning involves each student of the class, doing the same exact thing as his or her classmates. Too early in their lives many students give up on education, because a couple of students are the "smart" ones with all the right answers first. Or they come to learn that thinking is not what gets you called smart in school; just memorizing answers for the most part—the same as everyone else.

If we break down enough educational barriers, we can also undo a lot of the effect of what class you are born into. Your ability to excel won't be determined by which school you attend. It will be a more equal playing field. But we can't lose students at age 8 who decide that education isn't their strong point. Things like today's grading methods get in the way. Letting every student take as much time on anything they want to learn to reach A+ status will keep so many from dropping out by high school.

Hopefully, in the future, learners will have the opportunity to develop the skills needed to exploit all this random information and apply it to solve real-world problems. The tools on this path will include programming and communication skills, along with multimedia talents. Words can say so much, but the way ideas are presented to others is what amounts to real communication. These are the skills that should be emphasized in schools of the future. The future?

The future is here today.

This is exactly what Ian and Ryan examine in *A Brief History of the Future of Education*. They consider the unconscious mindsets we are so comfortable in maintaining, and how change can sneak up on us and give us a swift kick in the assumptions. The challenge we face is that change is inevitable, sneaky, disruptive, and accelerating.

Reprogramming education to reflect modern times requires schools to embrace the challenge of change by supporting today's learners and leveraging their passions and digital learning preferences. It's time for education to refocus its energies into helping our learners develop the essential next-generation skills and habits of mind they will need to thrive in modern times. That's what this book is all about. Enjoy!!!

—Steve Wozniak

Steve Wozniak is an inventor, electronics engineer, programmer, philanthropist, teacher, and technology entrepreneur who, together with Steve Jobs, co-founded Apple Inc. He is known as the inventor of the personal computer, as well as the first universal remote control. Some of his many awards and accolades include the National Medal of Technology, induction into the Inventors and the Consumer Electronics Halls of Fame, and a Hoover, Heinz, and Isaac Asimov Science Award. He is currently reprogramming educational thinking with the launch of his personalized learning service Woz U. In his "spare" time, Steve was part of the team that created Segway Polo.

ACKNOWLEDGMENTS

Ian wishes to thank his colleagues Glenn Nowosad, Dr. Brian Chinni, Frank Kelly, Andy Rankin, Michael Strahan, George Saltsman, Dr. Fran Murphy, and Dr. Bob Thompson for their guidance, encouragement, and, above all, friendship. And to Ryan—thanks for your endless persistence and optimism.

Ryan commends the faculty and students of Notre Dame of Maryland University for their mission to transform the world. Also, a special thank you to Ian and Nicky for being such incredible colleagues and mentors. Finally, Ryan thanks the learners of today. May their futures be ripe with prosperity and creativity.

A special thanks to Steve and Janet Wozniak for their patience, support, and understanding during the long process of getting *A Brief History of the Future of Education* to publication.

PUBLISHER'S ACKNOWLEDGMENTS

Corwin gratefully acknowledges the contributions of the following reviewers:

Clint R. Heitz, Instructional Coach
Bettendorf, IA

Kurt Nyquist, Elementary Principal (PreK–4)
Centre Hall, PA

Dr. Virginia E. Kelsen, Executive Director (High School District), Career Readiness
Ontario, CA

Dr. Emily McCarren, High School Principal
Honolulu, HI

David G. Daniels, High School Principal
Conklin, NY

Dave Ramage, K–12 Director of Integration for Learning and Instruction at the district level
Pottstown, PA

ABOUT THE AUTHORS

Ian Jukes is the founder and executive director of the InfoSavvy Group, an international educational leadership consulting firm. He has been a teacher, school principal, district and provincial coordinator, writer, international consultant, university instructor, and keynote speaker. He has worked with clients in more than eighty countries and has made more than twelve thousand presentations.

First and foremost, Ian is a passionate education evangelist. From the beginning of his education career, he has focused on the compelling need to restructure our educational institutions so that they become relevant to the current and future needs of the digital generations—and to prepare learners for their future and not just our past.

Ian has written or co-written eighteen books and nine educational series. His most recent books are *Teaching the Digital Generation: No More Cookie-Cutter High Schools*, *Living on the Future Edge: Windows on Tomorrow*, *Understanding the Digital Generation: Teaching and Learning in the New Digital Landscape*, *Literacy Is Not Enough: 21st Century Fluencies for the Digital Age*, *Reinventing Learning for the Always-On Generation: Strategies and Apps That Work*, and *LeaderShift 2020*.

To learn more about Ian's work, visit www.infosavvy21.com or follow @ijukes on Twitter.

Ryan L. Schaaf is assistant professor of educational technology at Notre Dame of Maryland University and a graduate faculty member for the Johns Hopkins School of Education. Before higher education, Ryan was a public school teacher, instructional leader, curriculum designer, and technology integration specialist in Maryland. In 2007, he was nominated as Maryland Teacher of the Year. Ryan enjoys presenting sessions and workshops about the potential for gaming in the classroom, the characteristics of 21st century learning, and emerging technologies and trends in education.

Ryan has published several research articles related to the use of digital games as an effective instructional strategy in the classroom in *New Horizons for Learning* and the *Canadian Journal of Action Research*. His published books include *Making School a Game Worth Playing: Digital Games in the Classroom*; *Using Digital Games as Assessment and Instruction Tools*; *Reinventing Learning for the Always-On Generation: Strategies and Apps That Work*; and *Game On: Using Digital Games to Transform Teaching, Learning, and Assessment*.

To learn more about Ryan's work, follow @RyanLSchaaf on Twitter.

INTRODUCTION

WHY THIS BOOK IS CALLED *A BRIEF HISTORY OF THE FUTURE OF EDUCATION*

The digital revolution has only just begun, but already it overwhelms us. We live in a new digital landscape that is overwhelming our ability to manage our lives, outdating our laws, transforming long-standing customs, reorganizing the economy, reordering our priorities, redefining our workplace, changing our concept of reality, and making us sit for ever-longer periods of time in front of glowing screens. As the world continues to change at a frenetic pace, so will education. That is the focus of this book.

Although we offer ideas and pathways for changes in how we educate the digital generations (those generations who've grown up in an internet-connected world), this book is primarily about accepting the reality of change and encouraging you, as an educator or educational stakeholder, to be willing to experiment and try new things with learners.

Ask yourself, "What is the future of education in a world where connectivity has and is fundamentally transforming knowledge?" Knowledge will always be important, but we live in an *age of InfoWhelm*, where information is instantly accessible, limitless, and overwhelming. Because of InfoWhelm, most of us now carry a side brain around with us all the time in the form of an internet-connected device. We constantly use our side brain to look up information and stay connected to our family, friends, workers, and interests. As a result, we increasingly outsource menial facts from our consciousness and focus more on application and creation than retention.

Many of us don't bother to memorize phone numbers anymore. We just tap on our phones, and they do the rest. We become paralyzed from digital withdrawal when a wireless network goes down. Our students are deeply connected, always-on learners whom the internet seriously, intelligently augments. These students take instantaneous access to information and around-the-clock connectivity for granted. To them, connectivity is a right, not a privilege—they wonder out loud why they must memorize the names of the countries and capitals of the world when they can find the correct answer online or with artificial intelligence in three seconds or less.

Anyone with an internet-connected device has access to the totality of human knowledge—presuming he or she can effectively navigate the mass data piles housed online. Rote memorization increasingly does not reflect the needs of our citizens or our workforce.

In light of this dramatic shift, educators need to understand that learners are our customers—they are our clients. To connect with them, we must be willing to come to them rather than expecting them to always come to us. We must treat them like customers and not servants, because learning is no longer defined just by a teacher and school bell.

> Learners are our customers—they are our clients. To connect with them, we must be willing to come to them rather than expecting them to always come to us.

WHY EDUCATORS MUST ADAPT

For the first time, there is real competition in education because learners have many new options for learning at their disposal—the most innovative ones don't even have the word *school* in them. To appeal to these learners, traditional education and traditional educators must work to understand, use, and compete with these other possibilities. We must constantly contend with disruptive forces such as mobile devices, social networks, cloud-based learning, learning apps, the maker movement, massive open online courses (MOOCs), gaming, flipped learning, personalized learning playlists, blended and hybrid learning, streaming video, and virtual learning environments to name but a few.

All of these trends are far more compelling, creative, relevant, and social for the digital generations than the traditional forced march through curricula that many learners continue to experience today. As a result, what we are seeing is the gradual separation of teaching and learning from buildings called schools. School will always be an institutional provider for childcare and socialization, but modern education is happening all over the place, and a growing percentage of it is delivered electronically rather than face-to-face in classrooms. In 2016, 5.8 million Americans enrolled in at least one online course (F. Smith, 2016).

Dealing with change isn't just a matter of educators being good at what we do; it's about what we do being relevant to the world outside of school and the present and future needs of our clients, who also happen to be our learners. If education is going to survive—and because adaptive technologies can already replace much of what teachers traditionally do, that is something of an open question—we're going to have to seriously and quickly up our game.

As authors, we will say more than once in this book, apps and advanced algorithms can't replace teachers—more accurately, they can't replace *good* teachers. The most powerful influence—the killer classroom app for the 21st century—is and will continue to be a great teacher. However, based on the way many teachers often spend their time, adaptive hardware and software can and will automate many traditional teaching and learning tasks such as delivering content, assessing learning, and communicating with parents (Arnett, 2016). Teachers who are only information dispensers, book readers, babysitters, and multiple-choice-quiz givers will have their jobs automated and ultimately eliminated in the same way that it has happened to both white-collar and blue-collar workers in the modern global workforce. Education researcher Thomas Arnett (2016) writes,

> The teaching profession is not immune to the effects of scientific and technological progress. Today's students often find that it is much quicker and more convenient to throw their questions at Google than to make time for dialogue with a teacher. The resources available online include not just a list of hyperlinks to text-based websites, but also videos, interactive simulations, and games that rival teachers' abilities to make learning engaging, fun, and memorable. New learning platforms, such as Khan Academy, make it easier for students to find educational resources that match what they are trying to learn. And at the cutting edge of edtech, cognitive tutors and adaptive learning technologies can measure students' individual learning needs and then deliver targeted instruction similar to individual tutoring. Software has even started to grade students' essays with teacher-like accuracy. (p. 3)

How much longer will students need a school or a teacher to learn algebra or physics? We believe that teachers who are unwilling or unable to change will become extremely vulnerable to the shifts of an ever-changing labor market. Ask yourself these questions: "Will teachers who are only information dispensers, book readers, babysitters, and test givers find themselves automated out of a job? And if so, how soon?"

We hope that an increasingly automated education environment will free teachers for more human and emotionally complex interactions with learners, but there are some long-standing educational paradigms and unconscious assumptions that education and educators are going to have to overcome first. Part of that process means acknowledging what research already confirms: our learners are different—fundamentally different, neurologically different from those of past generations (Carr, 2010; Doidge, 2007; Medina, 2008; Ratey, 2013; Small & Vorgan, 2008; Willis, 2007).

As we examine in detail throughout this book, modern students look at and interact with the world through a unique lens. As a result, they learn in fundamentally different ways from those of their predecessors. To see why, consider how visual learning; social learning; the age of super-mobility; and big data, gaming, and personalization are changing the face of education.

HOW 20TH CENTURY MINDSETS IMPEDE LEARNING

Standing in the way of making education relevant for 21st century learners are 20th century education mindsets. We must keep in mind that people raised on 20th century learning, those both inside and outside of education, really don't understand what's going on in education today. Many parents, politicians, community members, board members, educators, educational leaders, and other decision makers are completely out of touch with how 21st century learners and even young teachers think, relate, and communicate. They don't understand modern teaching, learning, and assessment. Many of them think and speak using the traditional language of compliance because that was their school experience when they were growing up.

Generations raised on 20th century learning understand grades; behavior; some of the fundamentals of literacy; and other abstractions like effort, inspiration, success, and failure. But what if the older generations better understood how 21st century generations think and learn? What if the older generations understood the pros and cons of different instructional and assessment models, the inherent limitations of letter grades, or how to coach daily core 21st century skills like critical thinking, problem solving, and observation? The older generations are the sleeping giants of education. If they had any clue how poorly current education serves many learners, no matter how successful some learners navigate education in its current form, they would redirect the anger currently pointed at teachers and principals and superintendents, and point it instead at policymakers and politicians, perhaps even taking up the task of making the necessary changes themselves. It's critical that we take every opportunity to engage and inform these generations about what is going on because the futures of all nations are at stake. That is the purpose of the book and why we call it *A Brief History of the Future of Education*.

CREATING A MOVEMENT

The purpose of this book is twofold. First, it is to inform all stakeholders of the current state of education; second, it is to create a movement to move education from where it is to where it needs to be. As stakeholders, we include teachers, educational leaders, technology learning specialists, parents, and all members of the wider community.

Teachers, young and old alike, will find here a description of the current state of school and education. Educational leaders will have to help create a vision to change traditional schools. Technology learning specialists will have to help educators and leaders alike in embracing tools to improve modern-day teaching, learning, and assessment. For parents, this book provides a better understanding of how different students in the digital generations are and strategies to help them become lifelong learners. For the community members who are part of the modern-day workforce and anyone else, this book becomes a road map to the future of education.

Chapter 1 defines "That's the Way We've Always Done It" (TTWWADI) and examines TTWWADI's current impact on schools. **Chapter 2** is a wake-up call to the scary and often-sneaky nature of change in our world and how a broad, fixed mindset in schools is a troubling situation. **Chapter 3** explores how many modern-day innovations disrupt markets, business, communities, or societies and what these disruptions mean for the digital generations and the schools that claim to prepare them for a brave new world. **Chapter 4** investigates how learners who are ever under digital bombardment prefer to learn and how teaching must account for those preferences. We also offer some helpful instructional strategies, tools, and resources to access these learning tendencies. **Chapter 5** provides a workshop-level set of experiences to prepare readers to accept change and open their minds to the future of education. **Chapter 6** presents a preview of a student going to school twenty years in the future. We follow up her experience with eleven predictions about the future of learning. **Chapter 7** explains how we as educators can have it all—address academic standards, address content, and prepare for standardized tests while simultaneously cultivating modern-day learning skills. **Chapter 8** analyzes eleven critical roles that educators must embrace to prepare their learners for the future and provide them with resources and professional outlets to prepare for these new roles. Finally, the closing **epilogue** challenges readers to change their schools to prepare students for their futures and not our past. It uses an analogy about *committed sardines* as a call to action for educators and change agents to immediately reform schools to create the global citizens we desperately need—now and tomorrow. Each chapter concludes with a link to a digital resource collection associated with the chapter's content, a summary of the chapter's main points, and a series of questions to prompt discussion.

As the philosopher Eric Hoffer writes, "In times of radical change, the learners inherit the earth while the learned find themselves perfectly equipped for a world that no longer exists" (as cited in Stanton, 2013). Our greatest fear is that despite our very best intentions to do what's right for our learners, we're instead doing a great job of preparing our learners for yesterday rather than tomorrow.

Our hope is this book will address the first obstacle by helping you become aware of what's going on in the world outside of education and why it is so critical that we respond. We face a depth and breadth of change unparalleled since the Industrial Revolution. The old values and institutions are breaking up, and we're unsure what will replace them. Change either happens to us or despite us. Are we going to deny the changes that are happening? Are we going to resist them? Or are we going to accept the fact that we too must change?

It's time to stop asking what will happen if we do make the necessary changes and start asking what will happen if we don't. We get only one chance.

HOW TO APPROACH THIS BOOK

Do you remember the *choose-your-own-adventure* stories from your childhood (if you are young, ask your parents)? The books asked you to select from a variety of choices in order to progress to the next part of the story. They allowed readers to decide the next step.

You can choose to read this book by starting at the beginning and reading until the end—the left-to-right, top-to-bottom, beginning-to-end, page-after-page method. If that strategy works for you, great! Alternatively, you can opt for the choose-your-own-adventure approach—a strategy that closely aligns with the way in which many members of the digital generations prefer to learn. Your entry point can be anywhere you want it to be. You can skim or scour the table of contents, or search the book itself for a topic you find interesting, relevant, or required. Once you identify a starting point, feel free to jump right in. For example, if you are a classroom teacher facing the challenges of distracted and disengaged learners, you might want to jump directly to Chapter 4, "The Nine Core Learning Attributes of Digital Generations," and continue examining the areas pertaining to modern-day teaching, learning, and assessment in the classroom that you will find in Chapters 6, 7, and 8.

If you are a parent, we recommend starting at the very beginning to examine TTWWADI, traditional mindsets, and learning in an age of disruptive innovation. These are topics that will appeal to parents and all of education's major stakeholders—learners, educators, and change agents—because they begin at the macro level and narrow down to the micro level.

We offer these variable reading strategies to empower you to experience the text in a way that meets your needs. Regardless, this book will be an easy read. The chapters are contiguous in that there is a natural progression, yet at the same time, each also stands alone. Although we cross-reference content when necessary to provide avenues to further reading or review, we wrote each chapter independently of other chapters. Sometimes this means revisiting ideas across multiple chapters, but in each chapter, we are careful to approach these ideas from fresh perspectives and provide insights from new angles.

The time is now to better prepare students for their futures rather than our past. This book will help you make this essential leap!

1

BEYOND "THAT'S THE WAY WE'VE ALWAYS DONE IT"

The reason nothing important changes in education is because if one significant change is made, everything would have to change.

—Ted Sizer

IT is amazing how often people embrace doing things the way they have always done them without first carefully examining how or why a process came into use in the first place. We often accept a preexisting mindset because it is the path of least resistance. The mindset about the way educators organize schools is based on decisions made at the time of the horse and buggy,

oil lamps, and factory production lines (Lapidos, 2007; Wagner & Dintersmith, 2015). Continuing to operate with that mindset is a classic case of *that's the way we've always done it* (TTWWADI).

Schools haven't structurally changed that much in a long time. But the world we live in is no longer the stable and predictable place it once was. Disruptive technologies have ignited an engine of change, and that rate of change appears to be accelerating with each passing day. Radical developments hold profound implications for life as we know it. In an environment of constant and disruptive change, it is critical that we begin to question the rationale behind the TTWWADI mentality in our schools.

A PREAMBLE ABOUT FIVE MONKEYS

In his research, Gordon R. Stephenson (1967) finds that TTWWADI was evident in our evolutionary cousins—monkeys. Envision that you have an enclosure containing five monkeys. From the top of the enclosure, hang a banana on

a string, and place a set of stairs under the banana. Eventually, one of the monkeys will go to the stairs and start to climb toward the bananas. As soon as that monkey touches the bottom stair, you spray all the monkeys in the enclosure with cold water from a fire hose until you drive them away.

After a while, another monkey makes another attempt for the banana with the same results. Again, as soon as that monkey places its foot on the bottom stair, you spray all the monkeys with ice-cold water from the fire hose until it drives them away. Repeat this behavior until when one of the monkeys eventually attempts to climb the stairs to grab a banana, the other monkeys attack and prevent that monkey from climbing the stairs because they don't want to get sprayed with the cold water from the fire hose. Another attempt, another attack. Another attempt, another attack.

In time, the monkeys all become conditioned, and they understand that if they try to climb the stairs to get the banana, the other monkeys will attack them. Once the monkeys are conditioned, you can put away the cold water and the fire hose. Next, remove one of the original monkeys from the enclosure and replace it with a new one.

Soon, the new monkey will see the banana and try to climb the stairs to get it. To that monkey's shock and horror, all the other monkeys in the enclosure will attack the newest monkey because they do not want anyone to spray them with cold water. After repeated attempts and attacks, the newest monkey also becomes conditioned. The newcomer understands that if it tries to climb the stairs, the others will attack it.

Next, remove another of the original five monkeys and replace it with a new one. The scene will repeat itself. When the newest monkey tries to climb the stairs to get the banana, all the monkeys, including the first newcomer, attack the newest monkey, punishing it with the greatest of enthusiasm! Likewise, this happens when you replace the third original monkey with a new one and then the fourth and fifth.

Every time the newest monkey tries to climb the stairs, the others attack it. Interestingly, the monkeys that are beating the newest monkey have no idea why they are not permitted to climb the stairs to get a banana, nor why they are beating the newest monkey.

After replacing all the original monkeys, none of the remaining monkeys in the enclosure have ever been sprayed with ice-cold water from the fire hose. Nevertheless, no monkey will ever again attempt to approach the stairs to try to get a banana.

At this juncture, the critical question to ask is, "Why not?" The answer is, because as far as all the monkeys in the enclosure are concerned—that's just the way they've always done it. This is the essence of TTWWADI, and our superior human brains do no more to insulate us from this behavior than do the brains of monkeys. (Authors' note: No monkeys were harmed in the writing of this book!)

WHY WE DO THE THINGS WE DO

Do you have unconscious habits in your teaching practices? Do you ever stop to think about why you use a particular instructional pedagogy? Do you have the same rituals when you attempt to engage students in their learning? Do you have a routine as to how you start or end your class?

It is astonishing how easy it is for us to embrace doing things the way we've always done them without stopping to ask, "Why?" Often, this

> With all the effort required to think through an issue, it is all too easy to slip into a preexisting, fixed mindset. We choose to accept things as they are because it is the path of least resistance.

happens because it is much easier to continue going in the same direction than it is to reexamine the situation and reevaluate a decision or process. With all the effort required to think through an issue, it is all too easy to slip into a preexisting, fixed mindset. We choose to accept things as they are because it is the path of least resistance. In this section, we examine the true story of how Roman chariots dictated the dimensions of our modern railways and even influenced America's space program. This exploration does not specifically relate to education and instruction, but it does crystallize our collective human tendency to live with established practices because it's easier than changing them.

THE MINDSET OF RAILWAYS

Before we reach back to Roman times, let's start in the middle of the story. In the United States and many other parts of the world, the spacing between the rails on railroad tracks is a set standard—it is exactly 4 feet, 8½ inches (1.4351 meters). Now, some people might say 4 feet, 8½ inches seems to be a rather odd and seemingly arbitrary number. Why is it 4 feet, 8½ inches and not 4 feet, 6 inches or 5 feet, or some other random number? There are many theories, stories, and urban legends about this width, but the story that we like the best (whether it is true or not) is that 4 feet, 8½ inches was the track spacing that engineers in England used to build many of the first railroads, and it turns out that it was English expatriates who built most of the first U.S. railroads (Bianculli, 2001).

The reason England used a rail spacing of 4 feet, 8½ inches is that the same guild that had been building the horse-drawn wagons and handcarts in the prerailroad era in England also built the first English railways. It turns out that 4 feet, 8½ inches is the axle width the English wagon makers used to build the first railroad cars (Bianculli, 2003).

So, a question you might ask is, "Why did the wagon makers use that particular axle width of 4 feet, 8½ inches?" It turns out that they did this because they *had* to. If they used any axle spacing other than 4 feet, 8½ inches, the wagon wheels would almost immediately break on the sides of the established wheel ruts throughout England, which coincidentally also happened to be 4 feet, 8½ inches.

This begs the question, "Where did those old rutted roads in England originate?" It turns out that Imperial Rome made the first long-distance roads in Britain—and most of Western Europe, for that matter—more than two thousand years ago. They built these roads for their Roman military, and the roads have been in steady use ever since (Bianculli, 2003).

In fact, it turns out that Roman war chariots formed the initial ruts in these first roads; and it also turns out that the axle spacing of these chariots was 4 feet, 8½ inches. So, everyone ever since has had to adapt to those ruts to avoid destroying their wheels. Thus, it turns out the United States' standard railroad track spacing of 4 feet, 8½ inches actually derives (this is a fact!) from the original specifications for an Imperial Roman war chariot from more than two thousand years ago (Bianculli, 2003).

Now some of you might be thinking, *But that's stupid, that's ridiculous, that's absurd*, and you may be right. But here's the thing—specifications, bureaucracies, institutions, and systems have a natural tendency to solidify in their ways of doing things. Often, they may require people to do things in the same way their predecessors have traditionally done them, despite the fact the world continues to change all around them.

So, in this situation, a question you might find yourself thinking is, *What fool—what horse's backside—came up with this way of doing things?* In the case of the American railways, you'd actually be a lot closer to the truth than you could have ever imagined. Here's why—it turns out Imperial Rome designed its war chariots to be just wide enough to accommodate the width of two horses' backsides (Bianculli, 2003).

Indeed, it was a horse's backside that originally determined the way we continue to do things more than two millennia later. So, now we finally have the answer to the original question—TTWWADI! That's the way we've always done it!

SPACE TRAVEL AND HORSES' BACKSIDES

The story doesn't end with railroad track spacing and horses' backsides. Although NASA has retired the space shuttle program, when we used to watch space shuttles rocketing off their launch pad, there were two big booster rockets attached to the sides of the main fuel cell. These were solid rocket boosters, which NASA had made at the ATK Thiokol Propulsion factory in Utah (Bianculli, 2003). If you had talked to the engineers who originally designed the solid rocket boosters many years back, they would have told you quite categorically that they wanted to make those solid rocket boosters a bit larger to get more thrust and, therefore, more lift at launch. The problem was that they had to ship

the solid rocket boosters by train, 2,362 miles (3,801 km) from the factory in Utah to the launch site in Florida.

The railroad line from the factory to the launch site ran through various tunnels in the mountains. The tunnels were only slightly wider than the railroad tracks, and, of course, as we already know, those railroad tracks were only as wide as two horses' behinds (Bianculli, 2003).

So, what was obviously a major design feature to what was and continues to be one of the world's most advanced, sophisticated transportation systems—with more than a million moving parts at launch—was actually influenced more than two thousand years ago by the width of two horses' asses.

TTWWADI AND SCHOOL MINDSETS

In 1894, The Committee of Ten, a working group of primarily postsecondary educators from the eastern United States, recommended the standardization of the American high school curriculum (National Education Association of the United States, 1894). More than a century on, their recommendations continue to be the foundational principles upon which America's public education system rests (Wagner & Dintersmith, 2015).

At the beginning of the 20th century, agricultural-age thinking gave way to industrial-age thinking. Frederick Winslow Taylor's (1910) *The Principles of Scientific Management* became the basis for the modern assembly line. The employers of the time considered the factory model the most advanced form of organizational productivity possible. Not surprisingly, society modeled its schools after the assembly line factories of the early 20th century (Watters, 2015). It saw teachers as workers, the learners as products that schools produced, and schools themselves as the production lines. It designed schools to make learners into automated learning machines who would follow instructions that equipped them to play active roles on the assembly lines of the times—repeatedly doing defined tasks as accurately and rapidly as possible. Schools modeled after factories made sense for the time, but it also set in place conventions that are very hard to change.

SCHOOLS NEEDED TO LOOK JUST LIKE THE FACTORY

In 2018, we have an educational system intended to produce learners with the same efficiency and consistency with which Henry Ford built Model Ts (Watters, 2015). In the early 20th century, it made perfect sense for factories and schools to strive for standardized procedures, mass production, technical efficiency, and processes that could proceed at a uniform pace. This is no longer the case. World-renowned science fiction writer Arthur C. Clarke once commented that the difference between science fiction and science fact is that science fiction must be believable—because some of the reality that we are about to face is utterly unbelievable (as cited in Larson & Micheels-Cyrus, 1986).

Ray Kurzweil is a brilliant writer, thinker, and inventor with more than 3,500 patents to his name. Kurzweil has also made more correct (and documented) predictions about future developments than anyone else in history. Ray Kurzweil has made at least 147 predictions since the 1990s. Of those predictions, 115 have turned out to be correct; and 12 more have proved to be mostly right (off by a year or two), giving his predictions an astounding 86 percent accuracy rate (as cited in Basulto, n.d.).

Kurzweil says we are rapidly reaching a point in human history where what he calls the *singularity* will be upon us. Kurzweil describes the singularity as the point where man and machine merge (Grossman, 2011; Rejcek, 2017). As technology becomes more powerful, it becomes transparent—we don't think about it, we just use it like we use a pen or a fork. This transparency makes it increasingly difficult to distinguish between where human beings end and the technology begins.

Among Kurzweil's more notable predictions for the near future is his belief that by 2030 we are going to send nanorobots into our brains (via capillaries) that will create full-immersion virtual reality experiences from within the nervous system that will connect the neocortex to the cloud (as cited in Basulto, n.d.). The implications of this are difficult to overstate. In the same way that we can already wirelessly expand the capabilities of our smartphones by a factor of ten thousand by connecting them to the cloud, we will also be able to enhance our brains by connecting them to the cloud.

Let's digest that for a moment. The year 2030 is not far away. Kurzweil is talking about directly plugging our brains into the internet and being able to upgrade our intelligence and memory capacity by orders of magnitude. He's talking about brain-to-brain communications. No more email, tweeting, texting, phone calls, and so on—send your thoughts directly to someone simply by thinking about him or her. Imagine having instant access to the total of human knowledge at the tip of your neurons. You could immediately calculate complex mathematics equations, intuitively and flawlessly navigate the streets of any city, fly a fighter jet the first time, effortlessly speak and translate any language, or scale up the computational power of your brain on demand, making it ten or one hundred or one thousand times more powerful. Do you have to perform neurosurgery? Download the

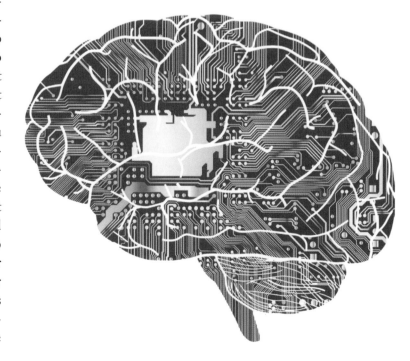

brain surgeon's software. In fact, you probably won't have to download it—you'll probably stream the needed expertise from the cloud to your brain.

We will be able to remember everything that ever happened to us because we'll store all our memories in the cloud, and we will be able to search a lifetime of memories instantly for useful information. When our memories become scannable, we will also be able to contextualize them by linking them with our calendars, important GPS coordinates, breaking news, weather, health data, stock market results, or anything else we might desire at that particular moment in time.

If Kurzweil is right, which he has been 86 percent of the time, what does all this mean for education when we can access any knowledge and integrate it into our daily thoughts? What does the future hold for education in disruptive times?

Sadly, very little in modern curricula reflects the astounding scientific discoveries we've seen since 1990, let alone what Kurzweil is predicting. Nor do today's instructional practices reflect much of the latest research on brain function and how it influences learning.

Why do we struggle with change while the world outside of education is changing at an accelerated rate? To make education relevant, we need to change and improve virtually every aspect related to how we teach, how we test, and how we assess and evaluate. Where do we begin?

CHANGE IS HARD—YOU GO FIRST!

We often forget how hard it is to change. Let's start by considering one bad habit you would like to break or behavior you'd like to change. Try something simple like stopping smoking, putting the toilet seat down, not saying "ya know" all the time, spending a little less money, or adopting a healthier diet. The big question is, how hard is it to break a small, bad habit? The answer is, it's *really* hard to change even small ones. Sometimes it's so hard that even small changes seem impossible, because change does *not* happen with one step or one decision. James Prochaska, a renowned psychologist, proposes that people hold great fear at the challenge of change (Ballard, 2016). He suggests that behavioral change is rarely a discrete or single event; however, we tend to view it in such a way. Often, behavioral change occurs gradually and over time.

When we ask educators and policymakers to change how they think about education, we are not asking them to change a small behavior like what we put into our bodies or how we spend our money. We are asking them to change some of the most fundamental, internalized, taken-for-granted parts of themselves and their belief systems. Changing an entire belief system makes the challenge of adopting a new exercise routine look like child's play.

A significant impediment to change is that the people who hire educators, the parents who attend parent–teacher conferences, and the politicians who write the laws don't want there to be any fundamental change from the way things were because that was not their experience growing up. It makes them feel uncomfortable. TTWWADI!

The definition of insanity is doing the same thing you have always done but expecting or wanting or needing completely different results (Einstein & Calaprice, 2013). If we continue to do what we have always done, we will continue to get what we have always gotten. This means failing ourselves and, in turn, failing our nations by failing our children. This is far too much failure!

To that end, we offer ten ways you can overcome TTWWADI mindsets in your schools.

Steps to Facilitate Embracing Change in Your School

1. Develop a shared school vision for teaching, learning, and assessment.

2. Align resources (personnel, funding, staff development, learning materials, and infrastructure) with your shared school vision for teaching, learning, and assessment.

3. Design learning opportunities that provide authentic experiences that are connected to real-world problems.

4. Reevaluate assumptions about what relevant curriculum is for learners.

5. Challenge teachers to become coaches and facilitators who promote new learning models.

6. Reimagine learning spaces to align with modern teaching, learning, and assessment practices.

7. Cultivate parental buy-in by encouraging them to participate as experts and to provide feedback on student projects and activities.

8. Develop a future-focused school learning community on students' future careers and life beyond schools.

9. Build teams of learners who collaborate on projects that create real-world products and solutions.

10. Make your schools places that embrace change and encourage continual reexamination, reinvention, and innovation that reflect ongoing disruption in society.

WAYS TO DEMONSTRATE TTWWADI

In considering how easy it is to fall into the trap of TTWWADI, we have curated a series of activities and anecdotes that demonstrate how infectious it can be and how important it is not to fall into it. These activities range from complex, multi-step processes to quick-and-dirty metaphors, but each should crystallize in your mind the ease of TTWWADI thinking and how it inhibits us from better preparing students for their futures.

THE PAPER AIRPLANE AIRPORT

One workshop activity we have used for years demonstrates the power of TTWWADI. Start by identifying an airport on a projection screen or use a box or trash basket. Ask the participants to design a paper airplane that they will

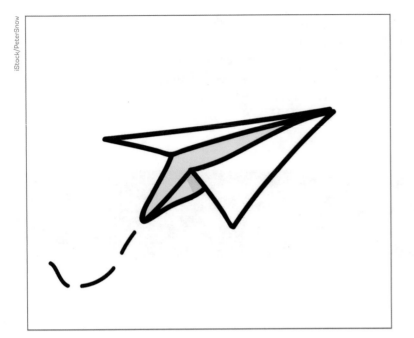

attempt to fly and land at the airport. When everyone has made an airplane, have them simultaneously launch their creations trying to land as close to the airport as possible. Typically, very few paper airplanes successfully land close to the airport.

Based on these results, ask the participants to rethink and improve their designs to make another paper airplane that will enhance performance and accuracy. While they are making this second plane, pick up the first-round planes and put them on a table to display. When participants are finished, once again, have them all fly their planes together at the same time. Often, the second round of flights is even worse than the first because many participants modify their existing paper airplane by adding more features to an existing design rather than designing new planes.

Collect the second planes and put them on another nearby table.

Now it's time to talk. We look at the first planes—every plane is different (paper, size, folds, and so on), yet it is likely that their creators based them all on the same paradigm of how to build paper airplanes. The problem is, most of these planes don't fly well, but that's just the way we do it. Teachers, like paper airplane designers, are required to do more and more these days, but like plane designs, schools do not change. We just add more features to them.

Then, we go to the second table to look at the newly improved planes. Many of them look interchangeable with the first attempts, just with more features added on. Frequently, they fly worse. TTWWADI!

The critical moment happens when we talk about the flawed mindset we use to design our planes and schools. Then we take a plane, crumple it into a ball, and throw it. This crumpled ball is inevitably a plane that flies farther and is more accurate than the complex planes the participants constructed.

> This crumpled ball is inevitably a plane that flies farther and is more accurate than the complex planes the participants constructed.

The point is, sometimes as educators, unlearning is more important than doing more to or for learners. We need to keep things simple and concentrate on what counts—how learners learn, not how we teach or administrate. With this thought process in mind, here is a list of five strategies you can embrace to place learners at the forefront of their own learning.

Strategies for Placing Learners at the Forefront of Their Own Learning

1. **Progressive withdrawal:** Gradually shift the burden of responsibility for learning from you to the learner where it belongs—the hardest working people in classrooms should always be students and not teachers.

2. **Velcro learning:** If you have only one side of a piece of Velcro, nothing sticks—you need to have the other side to attach to. In the same way, students quickly forget content taught in isolation, but teaching process and context at the same time provides the other side of the piece of Velcro. In our experience, when teachers take this simple step, students are more likely to remember content.

3. **Useful failure:** This is the process of letting learners fail in a safe space and assisting them to reframe their mistakes as valuable learning experiences. After all, Thomas Edison once said in reference to developing the first light bulb, "I have not failed. I've just found 10,000 ways that won't work" (Hendry, 2013).

4. **Future-tense thinking:** Push learners from a present-day mindset to a future mindset (James, 1997).

5. **Challenge belief systems:** Often referred to as epistemology, learners must have their outlook of the world challenged to broaden their understanding of other people's beliefs, perspectives, opinions, and values. By confronting a learner's views of the world, educators help them to develop a diverse, global understanding.

THE RUBBER BAND ACTIVITY

At the end of our workshops, we often take a heavy rubber band and stretch it out and hold it in place. After a short period, when our arms get tired, we release the pressure on the rubber band, and it snaps right back to where it was before. The question is, Why does it snap back to its original form? The answer is, because a rubber band has a paradigm, a comfort zone, a place where it has been for an extended period that it likes to be. In other words, it has a TTWWADI.

So how do you get a rubber band to stretch and stay stretched? There are several things you can do. You can wrap it around something; you can heat it, you can freeze it, and you can rub it with a solvent to change the chemical composition of the rubber. The interesting thing is that even after all that effort, when you release the pressure, the rubber band still tries to go back to where it was in the beginning. So, what has that got to do with education?

We all intellectually understand the world has changed and is changing. We nod and acknowledge that things are different. But, as the old saying goes, when the going gets tough, the tough get traditional. Without even being aware of what we are doing, we unconsciously revert to our old habits and beliefs (Ballard, 2016).

The rubber band effect occurs when our minds recoil from the discomfort of new ideas that are outside our experiences. We unconsciously and instinctively revert to the status quo. We go back to doing things the way we have always done them. When dealing with change, unconsciously reverting back to the way things have been done is a predictable phase that all people go through. You will experience this unconscious reverting today, tomorrow, or sometime in the future when you suddenly comprehend the true implications of new ideas like those in this book.

TTWWADI Digital Collection

Extend your knowledge of **common TTWWADI educational practices** by visiting http://bit.ly/BHFEC1. If you are interested in adding a resource to this collection of curated articles, contact us on Twitter (@ijukes or @RyanLSchaaf).

Chapter Summary

In this chapter, you read about TTWWADI and how it influences both society and education. As you reflect on this chapter, make sure you internalize the following key points.

- TTWWADI stands for *that's the way we've always done it*. It is a mindset that involves doing something the way it has always been done without examining how the original decision was made.

- Many schools accept a TTWWADI mindset of what schools look like because schools haven't structurally changed that much in a long time. Many educators embrace these entrenched ideals without question.

- Often, with a TTWWADI mindset, once someone makes a decision on a course of action, it is easier to continue doing the same thing over and over again rather than reexamining the situation and reevaluating the decision.

- Digital generations face a profoundly different world once they leave school. The current education model does not cater to the challenges this world presents.

- Schools and educators must now contemplate what world they are preparing their learners for. Schools should be preparing learners for the digital age, the biotechnology age, and the nanotechnology age. We need to help them prepare not for today's world but for the world of tomorrow.

Questions to Consider

- What is TTWWADI? How does a TTWWADI mindset affect schools and the decisions and processes that occur in them on a daily basis?

- Is there a school- or district-based practice or belief where you work that you feel illustrates a TTWWADI mindset? How would you go about trying to effect change in this instance?

- How do the paper airplane and rubber band scenarios illustrate TTWWADI? In what ways are these scenarios powerful analogies for some educational practices?

- How could a TTWWADI mindset in education prove problematic for the future?

- Why does education continue to struggle to deal with the challenge of change?

2

WHAT THE FUTURE HOLDS FOR OUR STUDENTS

Change is the law of life. And those who look only to the past or the present are certain to miss the future.

—John F. Kennedy (1963)

IN this chapter, we examine the increasingly rapid pace of change and how old mindsets persist even in a modern world. But first, we offer a quick story about change as it came to personally affect Ryan and his children.

Ryan's Perspectives on Change and His Children

I am the proud father of two young boys, Connor and Ben. When I think back over the years, watching them grow up is like watching a movie unfold in slow motion.

When my beautiful wife, Rachel, was pregnant with Connor (our first child), we tried to imagine what our "little man" would be like on arrival. Would he look like me? Would he act like her? One minute we were just a fairly new two-adult family, and then suddenly there he was—ten fingers, ten toes, and beautiful jet-black hair he inherited from his mother.

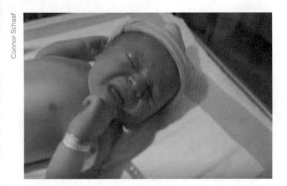
Connor Schaaf

We blinked, and before we knew it, Connor was a curious, energetic toddler constantly on the go. He loved watching *Handy Manny*, playing with his train table, and building with his LEGO blocks. He had problems sleeping at night and would always worry about monsters lurking under the bed. He would call out, "Daddy!" from his bedroom, at which point, I would stumble to my feet, stagger into his room, and fall back asleep next to him with my feet dangling off the edge of his bed.

Connor Schaaf

By the time Connor was five years old, he loved taking swimming lessons. Unfortunately, he would often get anxious during high-pressure situations. At his insistence, we signed him up for a swim team and then spent almost the entire summer gently encouraging him to race. When it was his turn to swim, panic would consume him to his very core, which led him to experience self-doubt and hesitation, and he would even break into tears. The same thing happened when he took up tae kwon do. We would have to drop him off and leave for twenty minutes until his anxiety had passed. Even flag football was a challenge.

In 2018, Connor is growing up quickly. His face has narrowed, and he has an athletic physique from all the years of sports activities. His panic attacks have vanished, and he has a real passion for swimming. He has also remained committed to studying tae kwon do and tested and received his first-degree black belt.

Connor and Ben Schaaf

When I look back over all these events, I am often struck by how quickly the time has passed. What happened to that little boy I watched enter this world? Connor's incredible growth is a living example of the relentless nature of change. We live in a time of change that is both subtle and sneaky. Where did the time go, and, more importantly, why couldn't I better predict the changes that I knew were coming?

AN OLD MINDSET FOR THE MODERN WORLD

As we see in Connor and Ben, we are beginning to glimpse accelerated gaps between the younger generations—between the brains of screenagers (a person in his or her teenage years or twenties who has not known a world without internet access), tweenagers (between teenage and younger years), and younger children (under age ten). Children who are four, three, or even two years apart are having entirely different experiences in the new digital landscape. As a result, even though they are all part of the *digital generations*, they think, process information, and communicate differently from previous generations.

> We are beginning to glimpse accelerated gaps between the younger generations—between the brains of screenagers, tweenagers, and younger children.

The students in the digital generations learned to type before they learned to write, and they use a keyboard more than they use a pen. Anyone who has seen a two-year-old playing with an iPad knows precisely what this looks like. Information and digital technology have completely saturated the younger generations' brains—that's why their brains are physically different from those of us raised in a predominantly analog world (Small & Vorgan, 2008).

The digital landscape is not new if you were born into it. Remember, an iPad is *the* most primitive technology that the younger generations will ever use. It is the pen and paper of their time, and it is the lens through which they experience much of their world.

For those who are part of what we call the *analog generations*, those generations who grew up mostly without internet-connected digital technology, society's organization kept children localized. Other than an occasional family vacation or a visit to see their cousins, most children had friends locally, went to school locally, ran around and played locally, went out to eat with their families locally, and shopped with their parents locally. They spent the majority of their youth within a few square miles of where they were born.

In schools, most of these same children spent their academic time learning the three Rs (Reading, wRiting, and aRithmetic)—five hours a day, five days a week, for one hundred eighty or more days a school year. In the classroom, teachers typically lined up learners in neat rows, and the learners used hand-me-down textbooks or listened to their teachers deliver content from the front of the classroom.

Upon graduation from high school or college, members of the analog generations got a job and, in many cases, worked for the same company for twenty, thirty, even forty-plus years. This stability and predictability were certainly Ryan's and Ian's experiences growing up. For these generations, parents repeatedly performed the same technical or cognitive skills day in and day out for almost their entire working careers. Research in 1983 bears out this experience, showing that, among workers aged forty-five and over, nearly one-third had been with their current employer for twenty years or more (Sehgal, 1984). Not anymore!

The modern workplace is a much more volatile environment than the world in which Ryan, Ian, and their families grew up. The challenge we all face is that society, people, and the modern workforce have changed while, structurally, schools have essentially remained the same since 1893 (Wagner & Dintersmith, 2015). Today, we have schools that are preparing learners for a world of the predictable and stable—a world that increasingly doesn't exist.

The great challenge we face is that we haven't so much as conceptualized the many jobs of tomorrow, because the problems they will need to address and solve don't yet exist. This is something that current data support. Since the 1990s, more than half of the new jobs in advanced economies have been temporary, part-time, or self-employed (Pfeffer, 2015). In fact, four-fifths of new U.S. employees are on short-term contracts—and this trend isn't going away. Research has suggested that 45 percent of the world's workforce would be contingent workers by the end of 2017 (Pfeffer, 2015).

What complicates this trend even further is that the skill set necessary for the modern workplace is constantly changing. In its *Future of Jobs* report, the World Economic Forum (2016a) states that 50 percent of all employee skills become outdated within three to five years.

Many schools and educators struggle with how to help learners prepare for living, working, and learning in a future workplace where the skills employers require are constantly changing. In the next chapter, we explore what it means for us to take a moment to consider how a world of rockets, satellites, mobile devices, brain research, robotic surgery, nanotechnology, and GPS (to name but a few) changes the needs of education.

Managing Change Digital Collection

Extend your knowledge of **how to manage change** by visiting http://bit.ly/ BHFEC2. If you are interested in adding a resource to this collection of curated articles, contact us on Twitter (@ijukes or @RyanLSchaaf).

Chapter Summary

In this chapter, you read about how old-world mindsets are holding education back. As you reflect on this chapter, make sure you internalize the following key points.

- The digital generations will inherit a world fundamentally different from the one in which older generations grew up.

- Understanding change over an extended period can be a difficult experience or, at the least, a very disturbing one.

- We are beginning to see cognitive differences between the younger generations due in large part to their experiences with advanced technologies. Children who are two, three, or four years apart have completely different experiences with technology compared to previous generations. As a result, they think, process information, and communicate differently from past generations.

Questions to Consider

- How do schools need to change to be prepared to teach the Connors and Bens of the modern world?

- Have you noticed that your students learn in a different manner than you did growing up? What differences have you seen?

- When they reach adulthood, what problems, challenges, and opportunities will students have to anticipate, address, and solve?

- How can educators, parents, and civic leaders help bring about the necessary changes in the education system?

- If you could change one thing in schools, what would it be? How would others respond to this change?

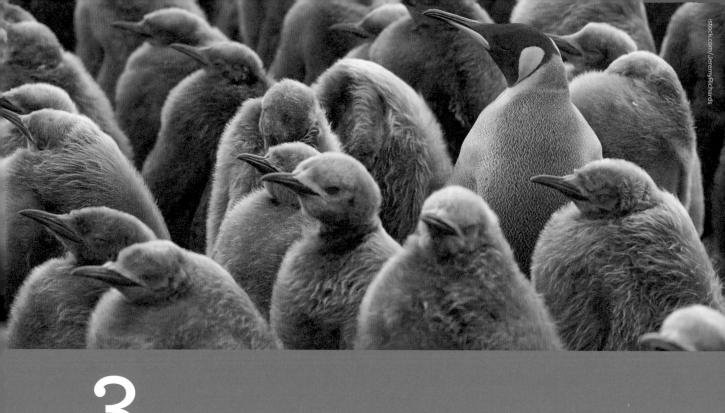

3
LIFE IN THE AGE OF DISRUPTIVE INNOVATION

Things move along so rapidly nowadays that people saying "It can't be done" are always being interrupted by somebody doing it.

—*Puck* magazine

THIS chapter is about change: change in our children, change in our families, change in our communities, and change in our world. The greatest challenge we face in times of accelerated change is that change is subtle and sneaky. We all know something big is happening, and it's easy to reflect on major hallmarks of change like the internet or mobile technology, but when we think about how these harbingers of change affect our society and our families and how we learn, it is hard to put our finger on

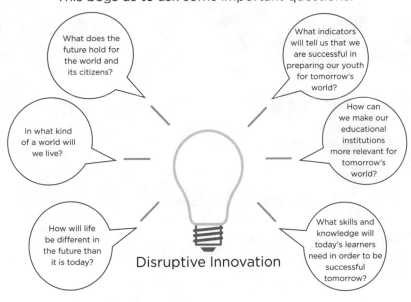

This begs us to ask some important questions:

- What does the future hold for the world and its citizens?
- In what kind of a world will we live?
- How will life be different in the future than it is today?
- What indicators will tell us that we are successful in preparing our youth for tomorrow's world?
- How can we make our educational institutions more relevant for tomorrow's world?
- What skills and knowledge will today's learners need in order to be successful tomorrow?

Disruptive Innovation

> Disruptive innovations are transforming the way we work, play, communicate, view our fellow citizens, and live in the world.

exactly what *has* changed and what *is* changing.

In their best-selling book *Disrupting Class: How Disruptive Innovation Will Change the Way the World Learns*, writers Clayton M. Christensen, Michael B. Horn, and Curtis W. Johnson (2008) introduce readers to the concept of *disruptive innovation*. Disruptive innovation is change that fundamentally transforms the traditional ways of doing things. Innovations such as cloud computing, big data, genetic engineering, smart materials, social media, biotechnology, 3-D printing, nanotechnology, artificial intelligence, virtual reality, and neuroscience are just a few of the big disruptors in the 21st century.

Disruptive innovations are transforming the way we work, play, communicate, view our fellow citizens, and live in the world. In this chapter, we focus on disruptive innovation; the skill sets digital generations will need to live and work in the modern world; and the implications that disruptive innovation holds for education, a new global economy, and education's purpose in modern times. In other words, we explore the driving forces of change—the *why* in preparation for examining the *what* and the *how*, which we do in later chapters.

HOW DISRUPTIVE INNOVATION FORCES CHANGE

Disruptive innovation changes everything in its path, and in a century where exponential change defines the time, the appearance of disruptive innovations is relentless. Whether we choose to acknowledge it or not, disruptive innovation affects virtually every aspect of our lives. We listed a swirling vortex of disruptive innovations at the start of this chapter, and these revolutionary changes are creating intense economic shifts; disorienting demographic patterns; forcing far-reaching cultural transformations; and globalizing every aspect of our world with enormous implications for communities, families, and the future of education. Disruptive innovations have fundamentally altered the working world to the point that it is all but unrecognizable to older generations. Let's take a closer look at what happened.

For the longest time, right into the latter half of the 20th century, the factory job and the factory mindset were the primary economic drivers—so prevalent that society modeled even our schools on the factory approach to instruction and learning. However, this model and the jobs associated with the factory mindset have been disappearing from the economy since the late 20th century (Long, 2016).

This is happening because disruptive innovations have made it possible for anybody, almost anywhere in the world, to do this kind of work. In the 21st century, where labor is the cheapest is not in places like the United States or much of Europe—it is in countries like China and even lower-wage countries such as Vietnam, India, Bangladesh, and Pakistan (Amadeo, 2017).

There has been one exception to this mass jobs exodus—that is, jobs that involve location-dependent work. Location-dependent work includes jobs in the construction and trade industries—carpenters, plumbers, electricians, metal fabricators, truck drivers, miners, loggers, barbers, cooks, delivery service drivers, auto technicians, restaurant workers, and cleaning staff, to name but a few.

All these so-called blue-collar jobs require workers to be physically on-site to do their jobs. Although many of these jobs face economy-dependent ups and downs, there is still baseline demand for these location-dependent workers. The same demand, however, does not apply to white-collar workers. (We write later in this section about the vulnerability of even location-dependent jobs to disruptive innovation.)

White-collar jobs are quickly disappearing from the economy (Brown, 2016). This is happening because powerful new software tools are disrupting traditional ways of doing business and replacing the need for many of these jobs. Digital tools make it possible for far fewer workers to do much more work, and even when software tools aren't replacing white-collar employees, these workers are at risk of their companies outsourcing their jobs to low-wage countries. The reason employers can outsource this work is that many tasks white-collar workers perform involve what we describe as *routine cognitive work*. In the following sections, we examine how technology is becoming increasingly capable of doing this work, how it's enabling employers to structure jobs as a series of gigs rather than full-time work, and how it's automating the workforce.

ROUTINE COGNITIVE WORK

Routine cognitive work involves repeatedly doing repetitive mental tasks. These tasks include work such as bookkeeping and taxes, data entry, call center work, reception, and help desk or customer support, as well as computer programming and legal research. Even the people who interpret MRIs and X-rays do routine cognitive work. In fact, if you have recently had an MRI or X-ray, there is a real likelihood the technician who analyzed it lives in a low-wage country like India or Pakistan (Outsource2India, 2016). In time, employers will likely assign that same work to robots (Meltzer, 2014). This is a trend that will accelerate as new innovations continue to disrupt. During the 21st century, routine cognitive workers must not only compete with people in the next city, region, or state, they also must compete with an extensive global labor pool of inexpensive but skilled modern workers and sophisticated machinery.

For example, the UpWork website (www.upwork.com) allows employers to assemble virtual global work teams on a project-by-project basis. At the UpWork site, there are millions of private contractors and freelancers from around the world who offer services in every imaginable white-collar work category. Even our company, InfoSavvy21, makes use of it.

We submitted an application to UpWork for a web designer, and within twenty minutes, we had more than 230 applicants from all over the world. We ended up hiring a fellow we identify in this book as Li Wei from Beijing, China. What you need to understand is that this individual could have just as easily been from Venezuela, Nigeria, Kuwait, New Caledonia, or just about anywhere else on the planet. In the new digital landscape, the economy is increasingly built on a global people network that is entirely internet-based. This rising collaborative economy involves working with people from around the world to solve problems—people who know how to leverage the globe, time zones, where work can best be done, and what skills best match the tasks employers need workers to complete. Rather than a single place of sustained employment, workers must increasingly adapt to a global gig economy.

THE GLOBAL GIG ECONOMY

People often think of networking as something that happens at a local level, but due to disruptive communications technology, this is no longer the case. The people network is global, and it is rapidly transforming the nature of work. As a result, in the United States and elsewhere around the world, we are quickly moving from companies of hundreds or thousands of permanent workers to businesses that employ temporary employees the same way we did with Li Wei.

This emerging phenomenon is known as the *gig economy*. The nature of work has shifted to include far more part-time, freelance, e-lance, contract, and contingent employment. Gianpiero Petriglieri, Susan J. Ashford, and Amy Wrzesniewski (2018) state, "Approximately 150 million workers in North America and Western Europe have left the relatively stable confines of organizational life—sometimes by choice, sometimes not—to work as independent contractors." Economic experts project that a growing percentage of the world's workforce is becoming contingent workers (Hoque, 2015).

We should also be clear that contingent work is not just about someone having one part-time job at a time. We're talking about people holding two to four part-time jobs simultaneously just to survive. These trends seem to indicate that we are nearing the end of the era of full-time employment that supports a person at a comfortable standard of living across a lifetime.

This is precarious employment, where there are few assurances of long-term or full-time work. As a result, many economies are quickly becoming nations of part-time workers together with all the attendant negative consequences such as inconsistent employment, financial uncertainty, and loss of job protection and long-term benefits. There are far fewer types of full-time work that have traditionally been the foundation of the middle class, such as drivers, website developers, legal clerks, photographers, accountants, and data clerks, to name a few ("Generation Uphill," 2016; Mulcahey, 2016; Murray & Gillibrand, 2015; Strauss, 2017).

We have already stated this, and we will continue to do so because this point cannot be understated—we all live in a very different world and economy from the one in which many of us grew up. Increasingly, the fundamental unit of the new workforce is no longer the corporation or company—it is the individual worker. Instead of workers coming to the work, increasingly, the work comes to the workers, whenever and wherever in the world they are at that moment—just as our business went to Li Wei in China. Disruptive innovations make organizing, managing, and collaborating with a global work team a simple task, and it doesn't end there. Automation, too, is massively disrupting the conventional workforce, and this trend will only continue.

THE MODERN, AUTOMATED WORKFORCE

The automation of work is another trend that we must consider when looking at the modern world. A report from the McKinsey Global Institute finds that employers aren't just outsourcing and offshoring work; they are also turning to automation, and this isn't just about factory work (Manyika et al., 2017). For example, every time you use the Expedia website to make a hotel reservation or purchase an airline ticket—or anytime you drop your mortgage numbers into the Fannie

Mae web form—what you have done is unintentionally and unconsciously taken away some frontline, routine cognitive worker's job. Think about legal software (http://lawyers.com), think about tax preparation (https://turbotax.intuit.com), think about online retail (http://amazon.com)—if an employer can reduce a job or task to a mathematical algorithm, it is easy for businesses to produce robots, microchips, and software that will do the job cheaper, faster, and often better. When that happens—*poof*—that segment of the job, or even the entire job itself, vanishes forever.

Consider that in the United States, beginning lawyers are finding it increasingly difficult to get jobs because people can get legal advice from IBM's Watson within seconds, with 90 percent accuracy compared with 70 percent accuracy of humans. The implications are staggering—there will be 90 percent fewer lawyers in the future; only specialists will remain (Equitas, 2016).

Also consider what has already happened at Goldman Sachs. In 2000, the investment bank had six hundred U.S. cash equities traders—highly skilled, high-income workers—on its trading floor. Today, it has two—backed by two hundred software engineers (Durden, 2017).

In the global economy, 80 percent of the workers primarily manage their own work, and employers expect them to continuously learn new processes, concepts, and applications (A. Smith, 2016). Increasingly, employers expect them to work in temporary groups of coworkers who collaborate on tasks that primarily require intellectual rather than physical capabilities. As a result, far more workers need high-level mental skills to harness the power of disruptive innovations to increase their productivity rather than just physical skills or routine cognitive skills.

Increasingly, no job that requires routine cognitive work will be safe in the 21st century. With rapid advances in artificial intelligence, computers and robots can do any task that requires information analysis both better and faster than humans. This disruption doesn't just include the jobs of office workers. This also affects even location-dependent work and not just that of factory workers. Automation is already replacing parking lot attendants, ticket collectors, restaurant workers, and bank tellers. It won't stop there. This automation revolution will eventually include the jobs of carpenters, doctors, pilots, language translators, and investment advisors, among many, many others—jobs that until recently required humans (Meltzer, 2014).

Consider Video 3.1, "Amazon Warehouse Robots" at https://bit.ly/2I7fdtw (Mind Blowing Videos, 2016). In this video, you will see an example of an Amazon warehouse floor loaded with robots and comparably few workers, which is quite a contrast to the traditional factory floor or even a factory floor from the end of the 20th century.

This kind of automation isn't restricted to production lines. For all the excitement over self-driving passenger cars, ships, trains, and airplanes, the truck freight industry is likely to adopt autonomous vehicles even faster. According to a 2014 Morgan Stanley report, full automation might reduce the pool of truck drivers by two-thirds ("The Elephant in the Truck," 2017).

There are 1.7 million jobs driving tractor trailers in America alone. Long-haul drivers now enjoy a wage premium over others in the labor market with the same level of educational attainment. In other words, if truck drivers lose their jobs, they'll be in particularly dire straits (Rotman, 2017). To get a sense of what drivers are up against, check out Budweiser's driverless Otto in Video 3.2, "Otto—Self-Driving Trucks" (Uber Advanced Technologies Group, 2016).

Even Uber, which has several hundred thousand active drivers, is investing hundreds of millions of dollars in driverless vehicles, planning to dispose with humans as soon as possible. Uber estimates that automated vehicles could threaten or alter 2.2 million to 3.1 million existing U.S. jobs (Rotman, 2017).

It is not just cars and trucks we are talking about. This includes trains, airplanes, ships, and buses among others. We believe, based on current trends, that driverless vehicles will be more disruptive than any other technology in all of history. We're talking about developments more disruptive than past innovations like the wheel, fire, electricity, filtered water, and sanitation systems—because the disruption will happen to more people in a shorter period.

But that's just driving. In July 2017, Amazon opened its first Amazon Go store in Seattle. Amazon Go is a 167-square-meter grocery store that requires no checkout lines—not even self-checkout. Watch Video 3.3 "Introducing Amazon Go and the World's Most Advanced Shopping Technology" (Amazon, 2016).

This automation revolution has not only freed many employees from physical labor in the workplace, it has also freed a lot of those same workers permanently from their jobs. According to *A Smart Move*, a PricewaterhouseCoopers (2015) analysis of an Oxford University study, the increasing automation of knowledge work means that, globally, employers may be free to cut two billion existing jobs by 2030. The report goes on to say that computerization and robotics will affect as many as 44 percent of current jobs by 2035 (PricewaterhouseCoopers, 2015).

For educators who want to better prepare students for this world, this begs the question of what skill sets will be in demand for this new, global economy.

SKILL SETS IN THE NEW GLOBAL ECONOMY

Let's pause for just a moment and reflect on the changes that we have examined to this point. We acknowledge that many of you might not like what you are reading and might be uncomfortable with these trends, and particularly you might not like what this means for you and your students or children. But whether you are comfortable or not, this is the reality we all face. Many national and international businesses believe that accessing the new global workforce is the only way to stay competitive (velocityglobal, 2017).

These developments have not only changed the nature of the workplace, they have also fundamentally changed the skill sets workers need to operate in these new work environments. Based on current trends, it is likely that people who need constant managing and direction will not just be unemployed; increasingly, they may be unemployable (Levy & Murnane, 2013).

Because of disruptive innovations, the very nature of work has fundamentally changed. We live in what Ryan and Ian describe as a *½ × 2 × 3 economy*. There are half as many workers that employers pay twice as much money, and those employers expect those workers to produce three times as much value using new digital technologies, software, and robotics. They expect workers to use technology to be significantly more productive than those who cannot use the power of disruptive technologies.

To be clear, modern workers are very different from traditional manual workers whose jobs focus on routine cognitive work. Modern workers are highly specialized craftspeople who have a repertoire of sophisticated new skills that make nonroutine cognitive demands on their brains. That is why the modern global economy provides very few jobs for the poorly educated. The days of well-paid, unskilled, or semi-skilled work are over. So, increasingly, the only choice for many of today's workers is that they either have high skills or they get minimum-wage jobs (Dobbs et al., 2012).

> Modern workers are highly specialized craftspeople who have a repertoire of sophisticated new skills that make nonroutine cognitive demands on their brains.

As Bob Hughes (personal communication, May, 1996), a former corporate director of Boeing, said at a conference some time ago, "Today, everything from the neck down is minimum wage." Everything that is only done with the physical body employers are now automating, outsourcing, or turning into software. Even high-skilled workers now compete against equally skilled, equally well-educated, lower-paid workers from low-wage countries. This means that the essential asset skill set of the modern worker is rooted in his or her creativity, and this has profound implications for education in modern times, as we detail in the next two sections.

THE RISING CREATIVE CLASS

Let's explore these ideas a little further. In his book *The Rise of the Creative Class Revisited*, author Richard Florida (2014) examines workplace trends in the modern world. Florida says we can essentially divide a nation's workforce into four basic groups: agriculture, working, service, and creative. In this context, we describe the creative class jobs as those professions that primarily require what we describe as *headware skills* and not just hardware skills. Headware skills are thinking skills—abilities such as leadership, critical thinking, problem solving, adaptability, productivity, accountability, communications, information management, creativity, innovation, global citizenship, and collaboration. Industry professionals often collectively describe these abilities as *21st century skills* or *modern learning skills*, and we talk more about these in Chapter 7. Consider Figure 3.1.

In 1900, more than 40 percent of the workforce was involved in agriculture. By 2017, automation reduced that number to about 1 percent. This reduction is mainly the result of machines replacing farmers and their work animals. What dozens of workers and hundreds of animals used to do, one worker and a machine can now do. Increasingly, driverless robot tractors replace even these workers, as do remote-control drones for herding animals.

The working-class group consists of traditional manufacturing, labor, fishing, logging, and mining jobs. These are the jobs that require only basic skills to

FIGURE 3.1

Job types as a percent of the global workforce

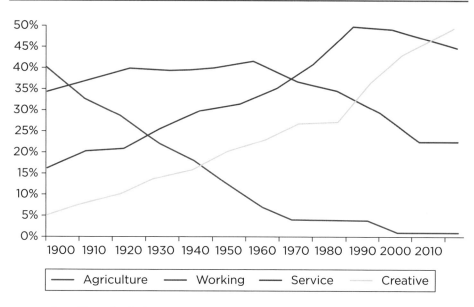

Source: Adapted from Florida (2014).

perform. The problem with having only basic skills is that as the economy has fundamentally shifted, advancing automation means there is far less demand for these types of workers.

The service group includes location-dependent workers and workers in service industries like hotels and restaurants. These are the people who do routine cognitive work. As you can see from the figure, these types of jobs peaked about 1980 and are steadily shrinking.

The final group is what Florida (2014) calls the *creative class.* These are the people who regularly do nonroutine cognitive work and consistently apply higher level thinking skills to their jobs. Consider Figure 3.2. You may notice on the right that the percentage of creative-class workers began exceeding the percentage of service-class workers in the workforce about 2008. You may also notice that since 1980, these lines are inverse trends—they are going in opposite directions.

This trend reversal began with the explosion in use of personal computers and other digital innovations, which started appearing about 1980; they have had an enormous impact on the workforce. Let us try to explain what is happening here: Technologies are *replacing* service-class jobs, while technology is helping *facilitate* creative-class jobs. This is because creative-class jobs require skills and expertise that disruptive technologies cannot yet replace. Although this is likely to change in the years ahead, to this point, technology can only augment or enhance these roles. Where things will go in future is a conversation for another day.

If we take Florida's (2014) chart and convert the data to stacked bars, it looks like Figure 3.3.

FIGURE 3.2

Inverted trendlines

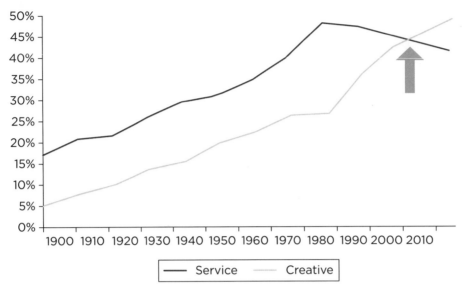

Source: Adapted from Florida (2014).

FIGURE 3.3

The changing workforce

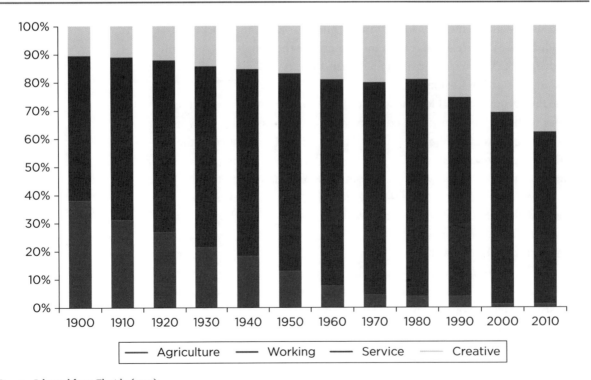

Source: Adapted from Florida (2014).

You see the steady decline of agriculture work in green at the bottom, and you see the continued growth of the creative class in pink at the top. If you look carefully at these data, you will understand why we face such a fundamental problem in education. Let's further examine that problem.

EDUCATION IN MODERN TIMES

As we established throughout these initial chapters, society built the traditional education model for a time when we had a very different economy, workplace, and way of life. It was a world based on three-quarters of the workforce being involved in agriculture, natural resources, and manufacturing. The primary skills in this society included basic literacy skills—being able to read—the ability to memorize—the capacity to follow instructions—and in many cases, physical labor skills (Wagner & Dintersmith, 2015).

As 21st century educators, we have to help learners prepare for a new world and a very different economy—an economy where three-quarters of the workforce is in service-class or creative-class jobs. By 2020, creative-class jobs could be as much as 50 percent of the workforce (Florida, 2014).

But why stop at the year 2020? Let's apply some exponential thinking and project job prospects for Florida's (2014) four classes of workers to the year 2050, when learners completing high school in 2018 will be in their fifties and those in kindergarten will be nearing forty years old. Let's see if this projection can give us any suggestions about the skills we need to focus on with our learners now (see Figure 3.4).

The implications of these projections reveal something incredibly important for the future of our world. What types of skills will our learners need to be adequately prepared for their lives and work in the modern world? What are we doing right now to develop these competencies in all our learners? Given that most prognosticators have the accuracy of dart-throwing monkeys when it comes to making predictions, it is impossible to accurately anticipate all of the possible factors and outcomes that might affect what the future world looks like and how it will function.

WHAT ALL THIS CHANGE MEANS FOR EDUCATION

Our challenge as educators is that while many of us recognize there is a problem, for the most part, our current educational system continues to promote traditional structures, traditional organizations, traditional teaching, standardized content, and standardized testing. With this TTWWADI traditional mindset, many educators continue to take every student's uniqueness and shove it into a one-size-fits-all funnel of traditional education, where we stuff learners full of information and then expect them to regurgitate back a series of single, right answers (Kohn, 2001).

FIGURE 3.4

Projecting changes in employment into 2050

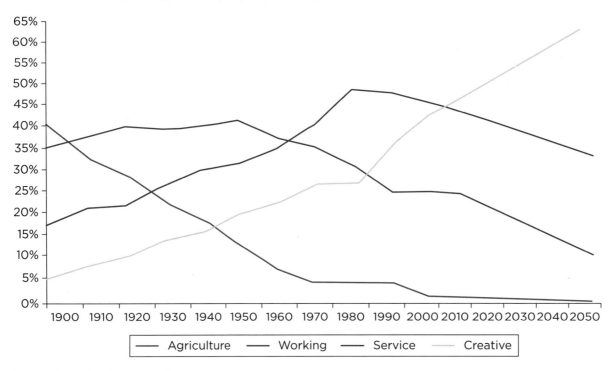

Source: Adapted from Florida (2014).

We are not being truthful to either our learners or their parents when we assure them that if the learners master the existing curriculum—if they memorize the content—if they do well on the standardized tests—that this is all they will need to be prepared for the rest of their lives. This perspective is particularly disconcerting when Richard Elmore's (2006) research indicates that between 80 and 85 percent of the work learners do in classrooms continues to focus on factual recall and low-level procedural thinking. In other words, teachers focus 80–85 percent of classroom activities on routine cognitive work—the work that employers are increasingly cloudsourcing, outsourcing, offshoring, and automating. We are preparing students for jobs and skills that are disappearing forever from the economy. Because this trend is a serious problem for all of us, in this section, we examine the challenge we face, the attributes of the modern learner, short-life versus long-life skills, and the dropout problem.

THE CHALLENGE WE FACE

The challenge we face, as educators and as a society, is that the subjects and skills that are the simplest to teach and easiest to test are the same skills that are the easiest to automate, digitize, and outsource. We need to stop thinking about success for our students only related to traditional test scores that rely heavily on teaching to a single correct answer and that primarily measure convergent and not divergent thinking. When we take this approach, learners may complete their education with certificates and credentials, but many of them still lack the essential competencies they need to be thoughtful, engaged citizens. Or, further to that, they lack the competencies they need to get and maintain good jobs in a rapidly changing economy, where a worker's value is no longer exclusively based on what he or she knows but rather the speed at which he or she can learn, unlearn, adapt, relearn, and apply.

THE ATTRIBUTES OF THE MODERN LEARNER

We often hear talk from politicians and industry about the importance of individualism, autonomy, and initiative. We admire creativity, ingenuity, and resourcefulness. We praise the self-made, the independent thinker, the school dropouts who make good. We know that capitalizing on individual skills and differences is essential for successful adaptation to disruptive change. But in the same breath, education continues to cling to a curriculum from another century that is designed to standardize learning. It is a system that marginalizes and diminishes those who do not buy into the traditional ways of doing things.

The gap between the learning that our learners currently do and what they require to survive in the modern world grows wider and deeper every day. Here are some strategies we suggest educators use to begin the process of preparing themselves and their learners for next-generation learning.

Strategies for Cultivating Future Skills and Habits of Mind Now!

- Subscribe to future-focused journals, blogs, and online communities such as Singularity Hub (https://singularityhub.com), World Economic Forum (www.weforum.org), Getting Smart (www.gettingsmart.com), Edutopia (www.edutopia.org), and TED (www.ted.com).
- Join a professional learning network such as TeacherCast Educational Network (www.teachercast.net), Kathy Schrock's Guide to Everything (www.schrockguide.net), The Teaching Channel (www.teachingchannel.org), Common Sense Education (www.commonsense .org/education), and Modern Learners (https://modernlearners.com).
- Participate in modern-day professional development from an online catalogue such as iTunes U (https://apple.co/QmukUS), Coursera (www.coursera.org), Udemy (www.udemy.com), or Woz-U (https://woz-u.com).
- Follow and read books by authors such as Gary Stager, John Medina, Tony Wagner, Peter Diamandis, Daniel Pink, Jason Ohler, Alfie Kohn, Sir Ken Robinson, Sugata Mitra, and Diane Ravitch.

To that end, Chapter 4 expands in detail on the traits of modern learners, with subsequent chapters focusing on how we can take advantage of their defining attributes to identify what skills they most need for future success and improve our instruction to match those needs.

SHORT-LIFE VERSUS LONG-LIFE SKILLS

Historically, the focus of schools has primarily been on *short-life skills*. These are skills related to memorizing specific content or learning how to use discrete procedures. Content standards, learning objectives, curriculum, texts, and pacing guides drive the modern educational world. We have a worksheet culture—we have high-stakes standardized tests, benchmark exams, and tests that drive instruction. These are all short-life skills. These are skills that quickly cease to be relevant, particularly when you live in an age of disruptive innovation and *hyperinformation* (massive quantities of information anyone can access from anywhere, anytime via digital devices).

The workplaces in the modern world, in the gig economy, place far more demand on *long-life skills*. Long-life skills are the modern learning skills that are valid now and will remain valid fifty years from now when the learners we have today are retiring from their careers. Long-life skills have no expiration date, so they will be as useful years from now as they are today. We explore these essential long-life skills in Chapter 7.

THE DROPOUT PROBLEM

It is our research-backed observation that many modern learners have disengaged from school and have either dropped out physically or mentally (Dillon, 2009). Although the numbers have improved slightly since 2009, in the United States and Canada, there are places where 10, 20, 30, and as many as 50 percent of learners have dropped out before they complete high school (Associated Press, 2008). For some people, that's acceptable. Even if those aren't your kids who are dropping out, this is not acceptable because the societal effect of students dropping out of school early include higher rates of poverty; greater likelihood of repeated incarceration; a higher probability of single motherhood; and the ongoing requirement of the expenditure of public resources for things such as prisons, welfare, food, and rehabilitation programs (Amos, 2009). These things affect us all!

Let us be very clear: learners are not just dropping out of high school. High dropout rates also apply to the learners K–12 educators see as successes—the ones who finish high school and then go on to postsecondary or tertiary education. Almost half of postsecondary learners drop out before completing a degree (Weissmann, 2012). In fact, Weissman (2012) reports that in some cases, dropout rates from postsecondary institutions are as bad, if not worse, than dropout rates from high schools.

Regardless of the level of education that individuals attain, society places an increasing emphasis on the essential lifelong learning skills such as critical thinking, problem solving, creativity, communication, and collaboration (World Economic Forum, 2015). Many learners drop out because they increasingly sense the absolute disconnect between our continued focus on traditional content, traditional instruction, and standardized assessment, and the constantly changing realities of living, working, and learning in the modern world (Gould & Weller, 2015).

CAREERS IN THE NEW GLOBAL ECONOMY

We live in a *Hunger Games* (Collins, 2008) economy where it's everyone for themselves—where the rules of survival are always changing—and where fundamental uncertainty and functional instability are the orders of the day. Analog generations lived in a world where what you learned once in your youth could sustain you for a lifetime and a single career. For digital generations, the idea of the forty-year employee who spends his or her entire career working for one company and in one career is a complete novelty. The cradle-to-grave security of the old company model is, for most people, a thing of the past.

Increasingly, the message people get from both companies and employees is that if they want long-term loyalty, they'd better buy a dog because they just will not get long-term loyalty from a company or employee anymore. Many of us have heard the prediction that modern learners should anticipate that they will have somewhere between four and seven careers in their lifetime. We think that's optimistic. In the 21st century's digital landscape, the new estimate is that the digital generations should anticipate having ten to seventeen or more careers; not jobs working in the same industry but distinct careers (Doyle, 2017). In fact, the average length of stay in any job for the digital generations is typically only between one and a half to three years (Carter, 2016).

Ian's daughter, Shona, is very, very successful professionally. She is in her midthirties and has already had ten distinct careers, ranging from banking to marketing to pharmaceuticals to the telecommunications field. What we need to stress to you is that, increasingly, Shona's experiences are becoming the norm in our world.

The challenge is that having so many careers requires learners to replace almost their entire bodies of knowledge several times during their working lives.

Having so many careers by the age of 40 is not something we should view as a sign of failure or lack of commitment or lack of self-discipline on the part of modern workers. Rather, as educators, we should explicitly prepare students to constantly manage their careers and always be thinking, *What is my next move? What skills do I need to learn tomorrow, next year? How are my talents best applied to the current situation? What is going to happen next?*

No longer can we expect learners to get everything they will need for their entire lives by attending school once in their youth. We are in an age where people must be learners for life who fall on the surviving side of the new digital divide—the knows versus the know-nots.

THE REALITY OF LIFELONG LEARNING

One thing we can predict with absolute certainty is that the knowledge students leave school with will not continue to serve them a decade or two later. Writer Thomas L. Friedman (2006), author of the best-selling book *The World Is Flat*, states that the skills learners need to be successful in university are a different set of skills from those that students require to be successful in life and work once they leave university. He argues that getting a four-year degree makes little sense and is not a good investment of time or money when, in all likelihood, the field will be radically different by the time the student graduates. Friedman suggests that, instead, the focus should be on earning a series of microcredentials and nanodegrees that take six to twelve months to complete, because what everyone needs is not a finite body of knowledge learned once in our youth but rather forty-plus years of ongoing learning, unlearning, and relearning.

Disruptive innovations are also causing fundamental shifts in in-demand workplace skills at an alarming rate. According to a World Economic Forum report (2016b), nearly 50% of subject knowledge acquired during the first year of a four-year technical degree is outdated by the time students graduate, according to one popular estimate. This trend means that workplace learning must become an essential, year-round activity. Lifelong learning is the only insurance policy individuals and groups have against being blindsided by disruptive changes.

THE NEW DIGITAL DIVIDE

For many years, people viewed the digital divide as a factor of wealth. Not anymore. The digital divide is increasingly a factor of education—the difference between the knows and the know-nots. To be successful in an innovation-driven economy, workers need more than just traditional skills like literacy and numeracy. They need core competencies like collaboration, creativity, and problem solving, as well as character qualities such as persistence, curiosity, and initiative.

THE PURPOSE OF EDUCATION IN MODERN TIMES

It is important that we emphasize that the purpose of education is about much more than preparing young people to thrive in the workforce. The purpose of education is also about the social, academic, cultural, and intellectual development digital generations need so they can grow up to be engaged, contributing citizens. It is not a matter of either/or, us or them, or our way or the highway. Education must prepare young people equally for life, work, and citizenship for the collective benefit of all the world's citizens, not just the survival of the individual.

Increasingly, employers will only pay workers for what they can do with what they know. This is a marked change from the past. According to Joshua Davis (2013), in 1970 the top three skills Fortune 500 companies sought were the three Rs—reading, writing, and arithmetic—whereas in 2013, the top three in-demand skills were teamwork, problem solving, and interpersonal skills.

Any nation's most significant assets are a highly educated, technologically literate workforce of lifelong thinkers and learners. These are learners whom schools have equipped with the ability to rearm themselves with necessary knowledge again and again throughout their entire lives.

Disruptive Innovation Digital Collection

Extend your knowledge of **Disruptive Innovation** and learn strategies for how you can better prepare students for an exponentially changing world by visiting http://bit.ly/BHFEC3. If you are interested in adding a resource to this collection of curated articles, contact us on Twitter (@ijukes or @RyanLSchaaf).

Chapter Summary

In this chapter, you read about disruptive innovation and how it is changing the landscape of work for which we must prepare students. As you reflect on this chapter, make sure you internalize the following key points.

- According to Christensen et al. (2008), *disruptive innovation* is change that transforms the traditional ways of doing things. Innovations in digital technology, cloud computing, big data, genetic engineering, smart materials, mobile commerce, social media, biotechnology, 3-D printing, nanotechnology, artificial intelligence, robotics, and neuroscience are disrupting how people work, communicate, and produce goods and services.

- Disruptive innovations have made it possible for anybody, almost anywhere in the world, to do many kinds of work. These types of jobs tend to be routine cognitive work, or work that involves doing repetitive mental tasks over and over.

- Society designed modern education for a time when we had a very different economy, workplace, and way of life. It was a time of predictability. Now, thanks in large part to disruptive innovation, educators must concentrate on cultivating the essential skills, knowledge, and habits of mind necessary to survive and thrive in the modern world.

- Many schools today focus on short-life skills, which focus on memorization of specific content knowledge or discrete procedural learning. Long-life skills are the modern learning skills that are valid in 2018 and will remain valid years from now.

- If education is going to stay relevant in the new digital landscape—if education is going to fulfill our mandate of helping learners prepare for their future—then schools must make fundamental changes. They need to begin to introduce learners to the skills and learning opportunities they will need to thrive as citizens, parents, and workers in the culture of the 21st century.

Questions to Consider

- Can you brainstorm several instances of companies or products that became obsolete thanks in large part to a disruptive innovation that changed a market or the expectations, needs, or wants of citizens?

- According to Richard Florida (2014), what are the types of jobs that are increasing in number? What is the forecast for these types of jobs in the future? Why must educators be cognizant of these emerging trends in the modern-day workforce?

- Why are headware skills so important for the modern (and the future) workforce?

- Why are long-life skills so important for the future of work?

- In days gone by, how would older generations view a person who had had ten to seventeen careers in his or her lifetime? Why should this mindset change today?

4

THE NINE CORE LEARNING ATTRIBUTES OF DIGITAL GENERATIONS

Do not confine your children to your own learning, for they were born in another time.

—Chinese proverb

EDUCATORS face the challenge of teaching learners who have never known a world without instant access to everyone and everything, anytime and anywhere. Digital games, YouTube videos, texts, tweets, Instagram messages, Snapchat posts, and all the other elements of the always-on generation's digital diet have created a landscape of experiences that are constantly wiring and rewiring their brains

> Scientists now have evidence that the brain's structure is far more malleable than we originally believed, and environmental stimuli, experiences, and emotions constantly affect it, causing the brain to reorganize and restructure itself.

and neural structure. Scientists now have evidence that the brain's structure is far more malleable than we originally believed, and environmental stimuli, experiences, and emotions constantly affect it, causing the brain to reorganize and restructure itself (Costandi, 2016; Doidge, 2007; Kolb, Gibb, & Robinson, 1998; Medina, 2008; Small & Vorgan, 2008; Willis, as cited in Sousa, 2010). We call this phenomenon *neuroplasticity*.

In *Reinventing Learning for the Always-On Generation: Strategies and Apps That Work*, Jukes, Schaaf, and Mohan (2015) identify nine core learning attributes of digital learners. These attributes don't apply equally to all members of digital generations. Factors such as access, culture, socioeconomics, geography, and personal or professional experiences can drastically affect the development of these new learning attributes. What follows in this chapter is a high-level summary of these nine learning attributes of the digital generations. We conclude each of these section topics with our recommendations for strategies, resources, and apps that support the new learning preferences for 21st century learners.

Nine Core Learning Attributes of Digital Generations

1. Digital learners prefer receiving information from multiple, hyperlinked digital sources.

2. Digital learners prefer parallel processing and multitasking.

3. Digital learners prefer processing pictures, sounds, color, and video before they process text.

4. Digital learners prefer to network and collaborate simultaneously with many others.

5. Digital learners unconsciously read text on a page or screen in a fast pattern.

6. Digital learners prefer just-in-time learning.

7. Digital learners are looking for instant gratification and immediate rewards, as well as simultaneously deferred gratification and delayed rewards.

8. Digital learners are transfluent between digital and real worlds.

9. Digital learners prefer learning that is simultaneously relevant, active, instantly useful, and fun.

Learning Attribute #1

Digital Learners Prefer Receiving Information From Multiple, Hyperlinked Digital Sources

Rather than being limited to the slow release of information provided in the form of classroom lectures, discussions, worksheets, or textbooks, modern learners can ask digital assistants like Siri, Google Assistant, Alexa, and Cortana for simple answers as questions arise in context. In the age of information overload (hyperinformation), it is essential for digital learners to master the ability to sift through and critically analyze all the data scattered across the digital landscape to discover the information they are searching for (and to disregard a lot of information they're *not* looking for) (Partnership for 21st Century Learning, n.d.). To effectively use the power of the internet, learners and teachers alike must be able to distinguish between information, misinformation, and

mythinformation among online sources. As educators, providing learners with information in multiple modalities and from multiple perspectives is key to engaging them as agents in their own learning and as savvy consumers of information.

Exercising Learning Attribute #1 in the Classroom

Many instructional strategies, apps, and digital tools help connected educators access this learning attribute with their learners.

1. **WebQuests** allow learners the opportunity to conduct online research using curated resources to solve a real-world application. By using many of the characteristics of problem-based, product-based, and inquiry-based learning, WebQuests promote a student-centered approach to teaching, learning, and assessment. Visit www.webquest .org to access further information and resources about WebQuests.

2. **E-books** provide learners with the opportunity to conduct in-depth reading and research. Although much of the current market of e-books consists of simple digital formats of hard copies, new e-book features allow readers to select hyperlinks to define vocabulary or research a highlighted topic in the text, watch slideshows and videos, manipulate virtual objects, or participate in discussion forums. E-books provide readers

with the opportunity to create personal learning journeys—they can experience the book by reading it in the traditional beginning-to-end reading manner, or they can stop and research a topic in greater depth for better understanding.

3. **Note-taking applications** like Evernote, Google Keep, or Microsoft OneNote allow users to organize and curate their lives using a single app. We particularly like Evernote, which is available for free from all major platform app stores and on the web. Evernote lets users enter content into notes. These notes can contain text, hypertext, audio notes, video notes, images, and files. Users can organize their notes into much larger collections called notebooks. In conjunction with a browser add-on known as Evernote Web Clipper, the software allows users to save entire websites with a single click (including functional hyperlinks). As you have likely noticed already, we used Evernote to put together the digital resource collections that we offer to support each of the chapters in this book.

Digital Learners Prefer Parallel Processing and Multitasking

It is possible for parents today to walk into their child's room to find him or her using a tablet or computer, earbuds draped around his or her neck blasting music from Pandora or iTunes, hands playing imaginary riffs to the song's guitar solo. Meanwhile, the child is also doing his or her homework, watching a YouTube video, sending a Snapchat message, downloading an image from Google, or searching

Amazon, all while simultaneously carrying on two conversations— one on Instagram with a person he or she has never met in the physical world, and the other one texting his or her best friend about last night's party. Meanwhile, another screen holds a paused game of Angry Birds. For those of us who were raised before the digital revolution, this scenario can seem utterly over-whelming. There's just too much going on at once! The amazing thing is, if you ask your children or students, many of them may tell you that they're still bored.

In his book, *Brain Rules: 12 Principles for Surviving and Thriving at Work, Home, and School*, John Medina (2008) states that research on multitasking indicates that contrary to what the digital generations might believe, multitasking modern learners are not nearly as effective at concentrating on a particular task as those who focus on a single task. In fact, Medina suggests that humans are biologically incapable of simultaneously processing multiple, information-rich inputs. The behavior the digital generations are engaging in is not multitasking but rather a demonstration of *continuous partial attention*—where a person randomly switches between tasks, decides which one to do next, and time-slices his or her attention into shorter intervals (Medina, 2008). Although the digital generations can't simultaneously engage in multiple cognitively demanding tasks, they can simultaneously perform everyday tasks they're familiar with or that aren't cognitively demanding. Even those of us who are a part of analog generations consistently engage in continuous partial attention—we're driving cars, listening to a morning radio show, thinking about a problem at work, reading a billboard, and discussing where we want to go for dinner with a passenger.

The digital generations use their digital devices to augment their thinking skills, and as a result, search results and instantaneous access to information are replacing lower-order thinking (Heick, 2018). In effect, digital devices are quickly replacing selective parts of our memory, while at the same time freeing up cognitive capacity to address higher order thinking tasks. As a positive, instant access to information and resources allows learners to spend time focusing more on the learning process than just the end learning product—these essential, modern-day competencies and character qualities are described by the World Economic Forum (2015), and we discuss them further in Chapter 7.

On the other hand, there is also growing concern about digital addiction. Although research is still quite limited in this area, researchers do find it is important for parents and educators to monitor how their children and students are using media (Domoff et al., 2017).

Exercising Learning Attribute #2 in the Classroom

It is important to understand that task switching must be kept to a minimum. If digital learners are performing more than one task at a time, it should *not* be cognitively demanding, *and* the two or more tasks should be ones with which they are already proficient.

1. **Have students work in collaborative teams** to engage in digital and nondigital jigsaw activities. By dividing instructional tasks among the members of a group, learners on each team can simultaneously perform numerous tasks. Although individual learners are not engaging in multitasking, cooperative learning strategies allow learners to break down tasks and projects into smaller chunks for them to complete.

2. **Allow students to use smartphones to access immediate information.** Many projects and activities in schools stall out when there is a lack of information. Having instant access to needed facts and information with the touch of a button, a hand gesture, or a voice command helps students maintain their workflow.

3. **Encourage students to use speech-to-text apps.** Applications like Dragon Naturally Speaking software from Nuance Communications provide a powerful, almost error-free speech-to-text experience. Speech-to-text allows learners to record notes, write papers, and control their devices using their voices. For some, this significantly improves productivity and allows for multitasking to occur in a digital environment.

Learning Attribute #3

Digital Learners Prefer Processing Pictures, Sounds, Color, and Video Before They Process Text

Traditionally, pictures are present in texts as a supplement to the intended message. However, due in large part to advances in and the prevalence of digital technologies and media, the digital generations have grown up in a remarkably visual world. Images have the ability to quickly communicate meaning. Burmark (2002) states that the eye processes images sixty thousand times faster than it processes the content of text. From an early age, modern culture regularly exposes the digital generations to television, computers, tablets, videos, and digital games that put in

front of children colorful, highly expressive, high-quality, realistic, multisensory experiences such as sight, sound, and touch. Based on current trends, in the not-so-distant future, we expect those sensory experiences will likely also include all five of the senses (Bloom, 2013). Most of these forms contain little, if any, text. As a result, many of the digital generations prefer to process pictures, sounds, color, and video before they process text. It's a natural conclusion that they prefer their media in the same way they use it at home.

Exercising Learning Attribute #3 in the Classroom

1. **Begin with images.** Educators can leverage the digital generation's propensity to embrace a visual world by adding visual media to just about any instructional content they use with their learners. However, these images must be high quality and colorful because they have to capture the attention of a generation of learners that grew up on video games, high-definition television, laptops, and tablets.

2. **Utilize video.** Video also continues to be a powerful instructional medium for digital generations. YouTube, TeacherTube, Khan Academy, and TED have millions of high-quality educational videos on just about any content areas, ready for learners to view.

3. **Teach graphic note-taking.** Another powerful method for learners to retain content knowledge during classroom discussions and presentations is to have them doodle images along with their text-based notes. W. R. Klemm, professor of neuroscience at Texas A&M, suggests that thinking in images and stringing them together into what he calls *story chains* will vastly improve how much learners can remember. Sketching notes makes these story chains visible and tangible (Klemm, 2014).

Learning Attribute #4

Digital Learners Prefer to Network and Collaborate Simultaneously With Many Others

In a 20th century learning environment, traditional educational practice is to initially have learners work independently before exploring what they had learned with their classmates. For analog generations, this occurred out of necessity, because communication options were not as prevalent as they are for the digital generations. For analog generations, outside-of-school communications with friends and peers were generally limited to conversations that were either made in person or by phone. The digital generations have grown up with literally hundreds of ways to communicate with one another. These learners can use digital tools to connect anytime, anywhere, with anyone.

The digital generations are highly social—although not in the same way that previous generations are. They use computers, laptops, tablets, smartphones, Bluetooth, Wi-Fi, video mashups, Instagram, Snapchat, Skype, Facebook, Twitter, texts, tweets, social networking, and hundreds of other tools to collaborate and learn independently or from one another. Based on current trends, being able to transparently communicate and work with others in both virtual and face-to-face teams is becoming an increasingly critical skill (Satel, 2015).

Exercising Learning Attribute #4 in the Classroom

There are numerous real-world and virtual tasks that promote opportunities for learners to communicate and collaborate.

1. **Teach learners how to be a model team member.** Help learners develop responsibility in team-based settings, assist them in learning how to create teams with equal roles for all, and provide them with the opportunity to be both leaders and contributors (World Economic Forum, 2015).

2. **Embrace collaborative, cloud-based platforms.** Cloud-storage platforms like Google Drive, Microsoft OneDrive, and Dropbox provide an ideal foundation for developing a virtual, collaborative workspace. In fact, while working at a distance of more than 3,000 miles (4,500 km) from each other, Ian and Ryan used Google Drive, Google Docs, and Google Hangouts to collaborate in writing this chapter. The experience of collaborative work is not restricted to word processing. Collaborating learners can create online presentations using Google Slides, a spreadsheet or database using Google Sheets, or a survey using Google Forms. Apple, Microsoft, and others also provide equivalent tools with similar capabilities. To facilitate speaking and interacting with peers, experiment with services such as Slack, Skype, and Google Hangouts, which offer users the opportunity to communicate across the digital landscape.

3. **Curate content and manage projects in Evernote.** Evernote is a mobile app designed for taking notes, organizing, making task lists, and archiving. The app allows users to create notes,

(Continued)

(Continued)

which can be formatted text, web page excerpts, photographs, voice memos, or a handwritten "ink" note. Notes can also have file attachments. Notes can be sorted into a notebook, tagged, annotated, edited, commented on, searched, exported, and shared with others. Learners can easily use these features to create virtual workspaces to organize content into workflows. In fact, the digital collection created for each of our chapters was created using shared Evernote notebooks. The app has numerous plans, but the basic account is free.

Learning Attribute #5

Digital Learners Unconsciously Read Text on a Page or Screen in a Fast Pattern

FIGURE 4.1

Z shape reading pattern

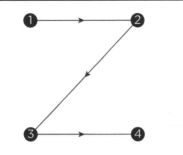

Source: Bradley (2015). Used with permission.

Because of digital bombardment and the chronic urge to rapidly skim, scan, and scour through digital resources, a new reading pattern has emerged in the always-on generations. Before the proliferation of digital screens and web-based content, traditional book readers engaged in a reading pattern similar to the letter Z (Bradley, 2015). Traditional readers start their reading experience at the top left of a page. Then, the reader's eyes read to the right until they reach the end of the text line. Next, the reader's eyes move diagonally down to the next line and repeat the reading from left to right (see Figure 4.1).

As a result of constant exposure to digital reading formats, reading in the 21st century involves viewing the layouts of things such as social media pages, websites, tablets, smartphone screens, e-books, and video games. Current research indicates digital readers don't read pages the way older generations do (Bradley, 2015; "Keeping an Eye on Google," n.d.)

FIGURE 4.2

F pattern thermographic heat scans

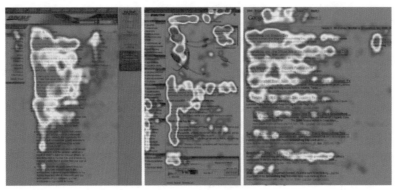

Source: F-Shaped Pattern For Reading Web Content" by Jakob Nielsen (April 17, 2006; https://www.nngroup.com/articles/f-shaped-pattern-reading-web-content).

Instead, their eyes first skim the bottom of the page, then scan the edges of the page, before they start scanning the page itself for information in what's called an *F pattern* or *fast pattern* (see Figure 4.2).

When reading in a fast pattern, cognitive behavior occurs as follows.

1. Users read in a horizontal movement, usually across the upper part of the content area. This initial element forms the F's top bar.

2. Next, users move down the page slightly and read across in a second horizontal movement that typically covers a shorter area than the previous movement. This additional element forms the F's lower bar.

3. Finally, users scan the left side of the content in a vertical movement. Sometimes this is a slow and systematic scan that appears as a solid stripe on an eye-tracking heat map. Other times, users move quickly, creating a spottier heat map. This last element forms the *F*'s stem (see Figure 4.3).

Consumption patterns aren't the only change we see in modern learners. With the emergence of digital media, reading itself has completely changed. Both children and adults just don't read the same way online as they do with paper. This is because there is a fundamental difference between reading paper and pixels, between reading and scrolling, and between linear reading and hyperlinking.

When reading text on paper, readers tend to concentrate more on following the text. When scrolling through information on a screen, the tendency is to read more quickly (and thus less deeply) than when we move sequentially from page to page with paper-based resources (Konnikova, 2014).

Reading using digital media such as laptops, tablets, or smartphones also speeds things up. On-screen readers tend to browse and scan; look for key words; and read in a much less linear, more selective fashion without stopping to ponder any one particular thought. This also affects students' ability to read deeply.

FIGURE 4.3

F shape reading pattern

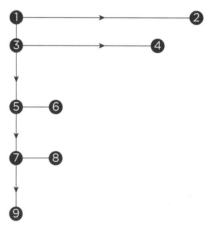

Source: Bradley (2015). Used with permission.

1. **Choose format wisely.** Select paper-based or digital resources depending on the type of reading you want your learners to perform.

Reading that calls for learners to analyze text deeply is best performed using a paper-based resource. However, tasks that require learners

(Continued)

(Continued)

to perform research should use digital, web-based resources for quick searching, accessing hyperlinks, skimming, and scanning.

2. **Understand the F pattern.** As we have moved from reading paper to reading screens, skimming has become the new reading. Understanding the impact of F-pattern reading holds enormous implications for the design of engaging reading materials that compel readers to read the entire page for meaning, rather than just a small portion of the page.

3. **Add images strategically.** Add images no matter what the medium. The human brain processes images much faster than it does text, so adding images helps draw readers in and create more connections with the subject matter. Since F-pattern readers tend to avoid the bottom and right side of the page, adding images unconsciously compels the reader's eye to stay on the page.

Learning Attribute #6

Digital Learners Prefer Just-in-Time Learning

Traditionally, schools use the *just-in-case* approach in their academic programs. Learners learn concepts just in case they will be on a test, just in case they need them for a good grade, or just in case they eventually need the concepts and knowledge when they grow up. However, as we wrote in Chapters 2 and 3, the world has fundamentally changed and continues to change even more every day. The global economy has created a new division of labor that rewards people who can make swift, well-informed decisions utilizing multiple information sources. At the same time, it penalizes those who lack the modern-day research and critical-thinking skills the new workforce and workplace require. As a consequence, learners are entering a working world where they need to continuously upgrade their skills to stay current—let alone move ahead—in their careers. The digital generations must prepare for a life of constant learning, unlearning, and relearning if their skills are to stay relevant in emerging work environments.

To be successful, schools must embrace a just-in-time mentality—just in time to learn a new skill, just in time to accomplish a new task, just in time to solve a real-world problem, just in time for a new job, or just in time to fulfill a new passion. When applied as a pedagogical strategy, just-in-time learning

iStock/LightFieldStudios

uses feedback between classroom-based activities and tasks that students complete at home, in preparation for classroom activities. The goals of just-in-time learning are to increase learning during classroom time, as a means of enhancing student motivation, to encourage students to prepare for class, and to allow the instructor to adapt classroom activities on the fly to better meet the individual needs of students (Macey, 2017). We explore this concept in more detail in Chapter 5.

Exercising Learning Attribute #6 in the Classroom

1. **Embrace scenario-based instruction.** Scenario-based instruction "uses interactive scenarios to support learning strategies such as problem-based or case-based learning" ("Scenario-Based Learning," n.d.). Since just-in-time learning calls for learners to have a real-world need or inner drive to learn, using learning scenarios places them in a position to develop new information or skills while understanding the context of that learning.

2. **Utilize online videos as resources for just-in-time learning.** Video-hosting platforms like YouTube and Vimeo provide an outlet for participatory culture in which more people contribute to content and produce content as opposed to just consuming it. If a person needs to learn how to change a flat tire, he or she can search for it on YouTube. If a learner must analyze the content of Martin Luther King's "I Have a Dream" speech, then he or she can call it up on YouTube. If a learner wants to supplement his or her readings of Shakespeare with video productions, then he or she can search YouTube for it. YouTube streams instantaneous information in the form of small video clips right to learners' devices just in time to save the day, just in time to learn a new skill, or just in time to explore their new passion. Learners aren't just consuming video segments, they are accessing them to learn new skills and solve real-world problems.

3. **Access your second brain.** Digital devices can be both a blessing and a curse. Although learners can be easily distracted by their use, digital devices allow instantaneous access to the global brain. Instant access allows learners to quickly search, gather, and filter multiple resources.

Learning Attribute #7

Digital Learners Are Looking for Instant Gratification and Immediate Rewards, as Well as Simultaneously Deferred Gratification and Delayed Rewards

Digital learners have not only grown up in a digital world but have grown up in one with advanced and matured tools to better navigate it once they get there. One of the most influential factors that keep them coming back for more is the constant feedback they receive from their digital habits. Digital tools provide instant and ongoing feedback to their users. This feedback provides them with immense and immediate gratification for their efforts. Why do they keep coming back?

The answer is simultaneously complex yet easily observable. If an aspiring photographer adds a photo to Instagram and immediately receives fifty likes from followers, then he or she is receiving both immediate feedback and instant gratification. If a young man shares a tweet on Twitter that friends and strangers alike favorite and retweet a dozen times, he receives immediate feedback and instant gratification. If a young lady posts a video on YouTube and receives seventy-five thousand views and hundreds of likes, then she receives immediate feedback and instant gratification. If a young gamer reaches Level 100 in his or her favorite video game, he or she receives immediate feedback and instant gratification. Says Jason Hreha (2017), a former researcher in the Stanford Persuasive Technology Lab:

> In most areas of life, feedback is either nonexistent or delayed. Throughout much of our education it takes days or even weeks for us to determine whether or not we did our homework assignments correctly. We're at the mercy of our overburdened teachers, and receive feedback only when they're able to grade our assignments. Tests are similar. It often takes two weeks for tests to be returned, at which point we can see what we didn't quite understand. Each of these feedback gaps is an impediment to learning.

Although these digital milestones provide immediate feedback to the digital generations, they also simultaneously provide deferred gratification and delayed rewards. Let's consider the previous examples through a less immediate lens. The aspiring photographer puts in the time to take the perfect photo. He or she may have taken hundreds of shots before settling on the best picture to share with his or her Instagram followers. The young man sharing his ideas on Twitter has to understand his audience and the type of content they want to read and tweet with others. A young man may be sharing a passionate blog post, an essay on tectonic plates, or a drawing that took hours to complete. The young lady has to carefully plan, record, and edit her video to make it appealing to the millions of media-hungry viewers searching YouTube for entertaining or informative content. Finally, the young gamer may have spent hundreds of hours to develop his or her video game skills and experiences to achieve a milestone that lesser-ranked players covet. All these examples are powerful representations of deferred gratification and delayed rewards. At the other end of the scale from instant gratification is delayed or deferred gratification. Delayed gratification is about developing techniques that allow individuals to be reflective and rational rather than reflexive and impulsive (Bazelon, 2012).

Things like smartphones, video games, and social media tools all tell the students of the digital age that if they put in the time, and if they master the game or tool, they'll be rewarded with the next level, a win, a place on the leaderboard, or a skill their peers respect and value. What they put into a task determines what they get out of it, and what they accomplish or discover is clearly worth the hundreds, if not thousands, of hours of effort they put into developing these skills. That is deferred gratification. But at the same time, the results of those efforts give students immediate feedback for their efforts and quench their constant thirst for instant gratification.

Exercising Learning Attribute #7 in the Classroom

1. **Allow learners to select their medium.** Student agency is a compelling aspect of learning—one that educators need to better utilize. By allowing learners to select the manner in which they express themselves, educators are not losing the opportunity to assess their learners for understanding. For example, an educator can evaluate the writing that occurs in a script for a commercial just as effectively as he or she can evaluate expository writing. Ryan's online list, *100 Things Students Can Create to Demonstrate What They Know* (Schaaf, 2014b), ranges from using audio recordings to making mock product pitches to designing a video game. You can find a link to the list on the book's companion website at https://www.teachthought.com/learning/60-things-students-can-create-to-demonstrate-what-they-know/.

2. **Use games as learning tools.** Learning through games (both digital and nondigital) provides learners with powerful learning experiences in collaboration and competition, while they simultaneously receive immediate feedback and assume ownership of the new information or skills they are learning. In fact, in a ThinkZone survey, over half of the administrators and teachers surveyed believe they can use games to teach complex and challenging ideas or topics (EdSurge, 2016). In a combined effort between seasoned educators, the InfoSavvy21 team collaborated to create the Digital Learning Game Database (DLGD; http://bit.ly/DigitalLearningGameDatabase). The team conceptualized this database to archive and curate digital games with learning potential and provide it to educators for use with their learners. The team categorized the database's entries by subject area, with summaries of the game and concept or skills tags to identify what the game helps to teach or test, and also categorized the games by gaming platforms such as web-based, desktop, console, or mobile markets (such as iOS and Android). The Digital Learning Game Database has hundreds of games for visitors to search through and is continuously growing, with the team adding new games daily to help educators deliver quality learning experiences to their learners.

3. **Use a bulletin board with a digital twist.** A digital frame allows users to add thousands of pictures to its memory. These devices allow the stored images to be displayed in a slideshow-type manner. Educators can use a digital camera, smartphone, or tablet to take pictures of student work. Instead of using a nondigital bulletin board that displays only a few working examples, digital frames can showcase learners and their work. Digital frames vary in size, storage, and cost, but are relatively inexpensive.

Digital Learners Are Transfluent Between Digital and Real Worlds

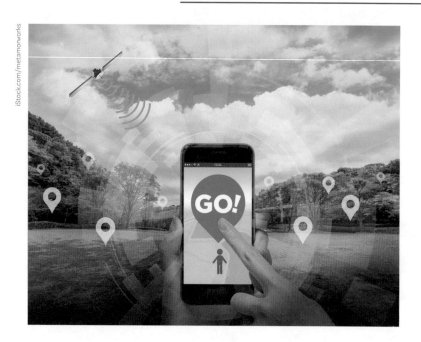

Because of the constant use of digital tools and regular immersion into the digital landscape, digital generations live a hybrid existence—one part constructed from real-world experiences and the other part a virtual environment. Whereas analog generations may develop a digital presence, many of them continue to see the real world and the digital landscape as two separate environments. "On the other hand, many members of the digital generations are transfluent—their visuo-spatial skills are so highly evolved that they appear to have cultivated a complete physical interface between their digital and real worlds" (Jukes et al., 2015, p. 121). For modern generations, their digital existence is just as relevant and impactful as their existence in the real world. Consequently, the digital generations have difficulty separating real from digital experiences. This is why cyberbullying has such a powerful effect. For them, text, images, and video viewed on a screen have the potential to cause equally as much psychological damage to the victims as real-world events (Schaaf, 2014a).

Fortunately, digital generations also experience many positive forms of digital interaction. For example, they conduct multiple discussions with friends and family members using virtual environments (often simultaneously) and regularly participate in activities related to scholarly or personal research, social activism, altruism, or crowdsourcing.

The perfect example of the power of crowdsourcing was the ALS (amyotrophic lateral sclerosis) Association Ice Bucket Challenge ("Ice Bucket Challenge," n.d.). During the challenge, eager participants engaged in a simple, temporarily unpleasant experience that involved pouring ice-cold water on themselves and sharing these experiences on social networking sites such as Facebook and Twitter. Participants engaged with the Ice Bucket Challenge to spread awareness of ALS as well as to solicit donations to fund research and clinical management projects to combat the disease. The Ice Bucket Challenge took advantage of the participatory nature of digital culture and was a litmus test that demonstrated the existence of a strong social fabric as well as a need to be constantly connected with one another.

Although the digital generations covet their smartphones and tablets, they don't think about them because they have outsourced parts of their brains to their smartphones—the devices are just a means to an end, not an end in itself. The digital generations use their tools to create seamless, transparent gateways between real and virtual worlds. They create unique and useful solutions to real-world problems by transforming raw information into new knowledge that they can connect to existing knowledge, which is the definition of transfluency (Jukes et al., 2015).

Exercising Learning Attribute #8 in the Classroom

1. **Take your students on a virtual field trip.** Many instructional strategies, apps, and digital tools help educators tap into their learners' transfluent nature. Great examples of this are 2-D and 3-D virtual field trips that provide an excellent opportunity to offer exciting experiences to learners who are eager to dive into learning that differs from the routine. Although real-world field trips are fun and we do encourage them, they can be quite stressful to plan and attend. Cost, transportation, and safety are also large obstacles to overcome. Virtual field trips tap into the power of digital technologies to provide enriching experiences for learners. Here is a list of eight virtual field trips to explore with learners.

   1. The Hershey Company (http://bit.ly/1lKN4bw)
   2. Colonial Williamsburg (http://research. history.org/vw1776)
   3. Global Trek (http://teacher.scholastic.com/ activities/globaltrek)
   4. Arctic Adventures (www.polarhusky.com)
   5. Smithsonian Museum of Natural History (http://naturalhistory.si.edu/panoramas)
   6. MPT: Bayville (http://bayville.thinkport.org/ default_flash.aspx)
   7. The National WWII Museum (http://bit .ly/2AtLxnV)
   8. Ancient Egypt for Kids (www.touregypt.net/ kids)

   Virtual field trips are truly immersive for learners and can provide an incredible transfluent experience.

2. **Embrace virtual and augmented realities**. Both virtual reality (VR) and augmented reality (AR) are starting to enter classrooms today. 3DBear allows students to create AR items and use 3-D printers to fabricate their creations. Star Chart allows users to see through a high-tech window into the whole visible universe. All you have to do is point your AR-enabled device at the sky and Star Chart will tell you exactly which heavenly bodies are directly above you. These change as you move the device from east to west, north to south.

   Google's Expeditions Pioneer Program provides a 3-D virtual reality platform built for the classroom. Google has worked with teachers and content experts from around the world to create more than one hundred engaging journeys—making it easy to immerse learners in entirely new learning experiences. Visit www.google .com/edu/expeditions for more information on Google Expeditions.

3. **Use social media for good.** As much as social media gets a bad rap, it's also a tool with great potential. Social media allows one voice to reach millions of ears (or eyes). Educators have multiple options to use the power of social networks for collaboration. Schoology and Edmodo are two social networks specifically geared toward schools, providing a safer avenue for virtual learning than open networks such as Twitter and Facebook.

Learning Attribute #9

Digital Learners Prefer Learning That Is Simultaneously Relevant, Active, Instantly Useful, and Fun

As educators, we must consider some critical questions. Will our learners remember performing the play *The Odyssey* for the student body? Will they remember the campaign undertaken to clean a local reservoir fouled with pollution? Will they remember the Skype interview they conducted with an astronaut from NASA, or a Pulitzer Prize-winning author, or a local politician explaining some of the important issues their town is currently facing? Or will they remember the countless hours of worksheets and homework you assigned as busywork? Will they remember the content of days upon days of standardized tests they endured before they graduated? Will they remember the content of the hundreds of stand-and-deliver lectures they received during their time in school? How many schoolteachers have ever had a former student return and tell them a question from a standardized test changed his or her life?

Digital learners benefit from learning that is simultaneously relevant, engaging, active, instantly useful, and fun. Ryan recently visited an excellent middle school in the Baltimore, Maryland, metropolitan area. The principal was excited to show off his school's makerspace—a dedicated space for students to use both digital and nondigital high- and low-tech tools to create—and student activities that involved coding. The experience was glorious; learners were engaged in collaborative work, and they had smiles from ear to ear. The room was abuzz with the noise of productive learners developing creative solutions to real-world challenges. Ryan left the classroom completely energized.

However, to his great disappointment, Ryan quickly discovered that this remarkable learning environment was isolated to a single classroom. As he walked through the halls, he saw repeated examples of teachers lecturing *at* completely disengaged learners. There was little evidence of interaction, collaboration, or higher-order thinking. Instead, many of the learners slouched passively in their seats, entirely disconnected from the experience.

As authors, we are not condemning this school. A single snapshot can hardly provide evidence of the efficacy of an institutional program. What we were curious to find out was why other classrooms weren't engaged in a similar manner to what was happening in the school's makerspace. Why was the engaging lesson Ryan had seen earlier an isolated example rather than a daily experience?

Outside of school, learners are constantly connected to others in a global intelligence. They are immersed in virtual environments that promote a participatory culture that encourages them to not only interact with their friends and classmates but also with others in far-off places. However, in many classrooms, learners continue to be unplugged. As a result, the digital generations, who have digital lives outside of school, might become resentful of having a nondigital life forced on them in school.

We believe this is important because, outside the classroom, members of the digital generations have a large measure of control. They pick what video games to play, what blog posts to read or write, what causes to advocate for, what videos to like, which friends to text, what music to listen to, or what passion project to embrace. However, in schools, many of the digital generations have little sense of, or opportunity for, ownership of their lives or learning. They lack the choices as to what books to read, what instructional tools to use, what products to create, or how to learn new information.

Exercising Learning Attribute #9 in the Classroom

1. **Provide time for genius hour.** Learners love the opportunity to study and explore their passions. Genius bars, for example, are an approach that allows learners to select their subject to explore and has them share what they have learned in a presentation or product (Carter, 2014). If a young lady loves butterflies, then she learns everything she can about butterflies and shares it with the world. With some reflection, educators can connect many of their curriculum's learning objectives to student self-directed activities. Educators can use the genius bar approach at any grade level, with only learners' imaginations to limit them.

2. **Offer makerspaces.** As we saw in Baltimore, the maker culture is another fun, engaging, active, and creative venue to explore with learners. With promotion from educators and tinkerers, the maker movement uses a variety of materials, computer programming, and inventive mindsets to create wonderful products. With imagination and hard work to fuel them, educators can immerse learners in a world of higher order thinking applications while at the same time immersing themselves in practical applications. After all, there has to be a fun reason to make a fruit like a banana into a computer keyboard, game controller, or piano (Blanton & Rosenbaum, 2013).

3. **Encourage role-playing.** Role-playing is a fun, versatile strategy that allows learners to explore their speaking and listening skills. A group of learners can write and perform plays, skits, dramas, or comedies that you or peers can record and publish for audiences outside the classroom.

INSTRUCTION FOR THE DIGITAL GENERATIONS

To be effective teachers in modern times, we must first possess the very same modern-day skills that the world expects our learners to have. These include being able to communicate, do research, think critically, and problem solve.

Combined, Ian and Ryan have accumulated close to sixty years of teaching experience. Despite this, both of us try to learn every day through engaging in professional development, conducting self-research, and listening to our learners.

Anyone who has felt the passion of teaching can tell you that the secret to success in the classroom has very little to do with being a good disciplinarian, classroom manager, or content dispenser and everything to do with creating engaging teaching methodologies that compel learners to *want* to be there. It's not about making learners learn—that would be the TTWWADI approach. It's about getting them to *want* to learn. If learners have no motivation to learn, there will be no learning. As an educator, ask yourself this question: "Would learners choose to be in your classroom if they didn't have to be there?"

We believe the most powerful technology in the classroom—the killer app for modern learning—is a passionate teacher with a love of learning, an appreciation for the aesthetic, the esoteric, the ethical, and the moral. A teacher who transforms his or her classroom into a nexus of knowledge, creativity, and innovation is a teacher that prepares his or her students for the world they will enter as adults.

It's crazy to think that almost two decades into the 21st century, we're still debating what 21st century learning is. Learners are *not* the disconnects of 21st century society. It is the institution that is the disconnect. Let's be clear: there's a place for traditional teaching; for basic skills and memorization; for time-honored, traditional learning. And just as we expect learners to respect and honor the long-standing traditions in education, we must also take the time and make the effort to recognize, understand, and engage with their world and their values.

> "There's a place for traditional teaching; for basic skills and memorization; for time-honored, traditional learning . . ., [but] we must also . . . recognize, understand, and engage with [students'] world and their values."

In our profession, we have to understand that the world has fundamentally changed and continues to change at a faster and faster rate, with no end in sight. What we desperately need is a balance between our world and theirs—between traditional and digital learning environments.

As you continue reading this book, the fundamental question you need to keep asking is: "How have I modified instructional assumptions and practices to address the fact that my students are fundamentally different from past generations?" If you or your colleagues haven't changed your teaching approach markedly in the past ten years, you and they are not meeting the needs of all your learners.

Chapter Summary

In this chapter, you read about the nine core attributes of digital generations and how you can better engage your students to embrace learning. As you reflect on this chapter, make sure you internalize the following key points.

- Learners today are vastly different from previous generations. New technologies and what we describe in an earlier book as digital bombardment have fundamentally altered the way the younger generations think and communicate.

- Digital learners prefer receiving information from multiple, hyperlinked digital sources.

- Digital learners prefer parallel processing and multitasking.

- Digital learners prefer processing pictures, sounds, color, and video before they process text.

- Digital learners prefer to network and collaborate simultaneously with many others.

- Digital learners unconsciously read text on a page or the screen in a fast pattern.

- Digital learners prefer just-in-time learning.

- Digital learners are looking for instant gratification and immediate rewards, as well as simultaneously looking for deferred gratification and delayed rewards.

- Digital learners are transfluent between digital and real worlds.

- Digital learners prefer learning that is simultaneously relevant, active, instantly useful, and fun.

Questions to Consider

- How has digital bombardment affected the way the digital generations think? How has it impacted the way they learn? How has it affected the way they view the world?

- How can learners and educators use visual media to develop powerful and compelling learning experiences?

- How has knowledge distribution changed from the pre-internet days to today?

- How must educators change their daily practices to effectively embrace the new tools and methods of modern learning?

5

HOW TO LOOK BACK TO MOVE FORWARD

Learn from the past, prepare for the future, live in the present.

— Thomas S. Monson (2003, The Church of
Jesus Christ of Latter-Day Saints)

THE emphasis on curriculum, standards, and accountability for all through regular testing makes it easy to slip into a mindset where we fixate on short-term results. We focus on the now. We focus our energies on getting learners ready for the next day, the next topic, the next school term, the next test, or the next education level.

We take the data from the previous year's test scores and combine them with the latest compliance mandates from the principal, superintendent, or our home country's department of education, and use them to drive our instructional decisions and learning strategies for the upcoming year. We examine the data and try to figure out how we can get our learners ready to perform better on that year's tests.

Year after year, grade after grade, curriculum revision after curriculum revision, we find ourselves in a never-ending loop where we check last year's test scores, look at the mandates, adjust what we teach, adjust how we teach, and then use that to determine which areas need more emphasis to better prepare our learners for this year's tests.

Please do not misinterpret what we are saying. Short-term goals are important for education. Short-term goals drive the day-to-day operations of our schools. However, education should not and cannot *just* be about a focus on short-term goals. Education is not only about getting learners ready for the next day, or topic, or term, or test, or education level. Education is also about long-term goals. Education is about identifying the skills, knowledge, and habits of mind that all learners need to have to be ready to succeed once they complete their schooling.

> Education is about identifying the skills, knowledge, and habits of mind that all learners need to have to be ready to succeed once they complete their schooling.

The problem is that we are still debating what 21st century learning should look like. So, whenever we meet with educators and school leaders, we always ask these questions: How do we have it all? How do we simultaneously cultivate both short-term and long-term goals? How do we prepare learners for the tests and, at the same time, also equip them with the essential skills they need to succeed in the modern world and new economy they will enter once they leave our schools? In other words, how do we simultaneously develop both short-term and long-term goals?

In this chapter, we write in detail how we can look back to move forward and then reflect on what the future holds if we accept a default outcome versus taking action. Finally, we examine the biggest problems that education faces and how we can overcome them. But first, let's start with a quick exercise that reflects how small changes in thinking can facilitate big changes that overcome obstacles.

What we did wasn't a matter of cheating. All it took was a tiny shift in our thinking that allowed us to go just a little bit further. That is what we are going to do in this chapter. We are going to try to go a little bit further. We are going to try to expand our thinking. We are going to take the handcuffs off our creativity. Sometimes, a tiny shift is all we need to solve a challenging problem.

We can take this concept to its next logical step by engaging in a game of sorts in which we first look back to 1998 and compare what life looked like compared to today.

Expand Your Thinking Using the Nine Dots Exercise

Part I

Grab a piece of paper and draw nine dots in a grid pattern as you see in Figure 5.1. Use a pen to connect the dots while adhering to these four rules.

FIGURE 5.1

The Nine Dots exercise

1. Start at any point.

2. Connect all the dots by drawing four straight lines.

3. Do not lift the pen.

4. Do not retrace your steps.

Some of you will inevitably have seen or done this before. If that's the case, and you know how to connect all the dots with four lines, your job is to do the same task with fewer than four lines, which is definitely possible. Work independently, or work with someone else, and take five minutes to solve this problem.

Most people, as we illustrate in Figure 5.2, start in a corner and draw a line to the opposite corner. Then they draw a line up one side. This is the critical point. What do you do from here?

FIGURE 5.2

The Nine Dots exercise, with two of four lines drawn

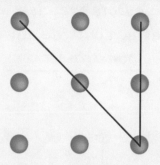

The problem we arrive at in this scenario is one of a self-imposed limit. We imagine boundaries. We assume constraints. We're focused on the nine dots, and because we're focused here, we see few choices.

At this point, most of us will begin to draw a third line as seen in Figure 5.3.

FIGURE 5.3

The Nine Dots exercise, with three of four lines drawn

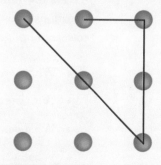

From here, it's game over—it's not possible to accomplish the task.

(Continued)

Part II

What if we instead focused on the possibilities? What if we focused on the opportunities? What would happen if we didn't limit our thinking? What if we moved beyond the nine dots? Figure 5.4 illustrates this concept.

Instead of thinking inside the box, we can expand the limits of our thinking and extend the second line just a little bit farther. From here, the solution is simple (see Figure 5.5).

FIGURE 5.4

The Nine Dots exercise, with a line drawn outside any self-imposed constraints

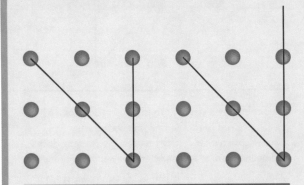

FIGURE 5.5

A successfully completed Nine Dots exercise

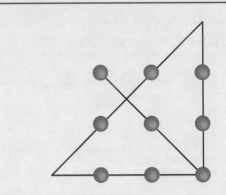

EXAMINE THE PAST TO LOOK TO THE FUTURE

Imagine you could jump into a time machine and travel back to the year 1998. Take a few minutes to identify and write down the answers to the following questions about that year. These aren't meant to be trick questions, so feel free to search online for answers to them.

- Who were the popular musical acts of 1998?
- Who were the major world, national, and local political figures?
- What were the major drivers of the economy?
- What were the major means of communication?
- What were the favorite new technologies?
- What were the characteristics of schools?

Many people quickly discover that remembering what happened twenty years ago can be quite a challenge. So, here's one that should be a little easier. Return to the modern era and consider the same questions we just listed.

- Who are the popular musical acts?

- Who are the major world, national, and local political figures?

- What are the major drivers of the economy?

- What are the major means of communication?

- What are the favorite new technologies?

- What are the characteristics of schools?

Make sure to write down your answers. Hopefully, this task was a little bit easier than trying to remember things that happened twenty years ago.

Now, compare your lists from 1998 and today. How many items from the 1998 list also appear on your modern list? Not many, we suspect. But why? Newer individuals, trends, and technologies have superseded the individuals, trends, and technologies that were prominent back in 1998. However, it is our experience that people regularly note that there are some very strong parallels between the characteristics of schools in 1998 and many modern-day schools. These include a continued focus on things such as memorization, content recall, high-stakes testing, and stand-and-deliver lectures. (TTWWADI strikes again!) How could that be? Twenty years have gone by! Meanwhile, most of the answers to the other questions have changed!

With all this in mind, let's take a look back at education and how we got here and then examine a path forward.

LOOKING BACK

Think about the changes that have taken place since 1998 and then complete this statement:

If we knew in 1998 what we know now, and we had made the necessary changes, modern schools would be different in the following ways . . .

Now, write another statement describing how we would have overcome the challenges of making the necessary changes:

We would have overcome the challenges of making the necessary changes by . . .

Note that this is a thought exercise, so there are no wrong or invalid answers.

MOVING FORWARD

Let's get back into our time machine and travel to the year 2038. Take a few minutes to identify the following.

- Who will be the favorite musical acts in 2038?

- Who will be the major world, national, and local political figures?

- What will be the major drivers of the economy?

- What will be the major means of communication?

- What will be the favorite new technologies?

- What will be the characteristics of schools?

Most people find looking to the future to be a real challenge. It is hard to visualize what things might look like even a few years out, let alone in twenty years. That should not stop us from gauging the possibilities and taking action, because whether we choose to take action or not, there is a future that will happen. There is a future that is waiting for all of us. If we do not take action, that future is called our *default future*.

CONSIDER THE DEFAULT FUTURE VERSUS TAKING ACTION

If we choose to do nothing—if inaction is our action—we still participate in the creation of that future. Our participation through inaction ensures the default future comes to pass. The default future occurs when we let change happen *to* us, instead of making change happen *for* us. The question is, Will we shape the future, or will the future shape us?

> The default future occurs when we let change happen *to* us, instead of making change happen *for* us.

Here are other questions to consider: Based on what we have said so far, what is the default future for our learners and our schools if we take no action and the status quo prevails? What happens if we play it safe and continue to approach teaching, learning, and assessment the way we do today? What happens if TTWWADI prevails?

Whether you think the future is promising or alarming, we want you to finish this statement:

If we take no action and stay the course, the future of education will be . . .

Now, we want you to complete this second statement:

If we take no action and teaching, learning, and assessment continue to be done the way they are today, the future for our learners will be . . .

Make sure to take some time to reflect on what you came up with and then consider how, if action is our action, we can create the future. If we are not satisfied with the current state of education, we can do something about it. The big question is: How? How do we deal with the future? How do we deal with rapid change? How do we deal with the fundamental uncertainty that is an everyday part of modern life?

We believe the answers to these questions lie in living life in split screen and thinking in future tense.

LIVING LIFE IN SPLIT SCREEN

If we want to anticipate the future, we have to learn to live life like a quarterback. Here is what we mean: when a quarterback steps up over the center, takes the snap, drops back to pass, and throws the ball downfield to the receiver, where does he throw the ball? Does he throw the ball to where the receiver is right now? No, he throws the ball to where the receiver is *going to be* (McCain & Jukes, 2000).

When the quarterback steps up behind the center and gets ready to take the snap, the quarterback is operating in split screen. One screen is focused on the here and now. In the here and now, the quarterback is watching how that 6′7″ (200 cm) 260-pound (120 kg) linebacker is moving around on the other side of the line of scrimmage. Above all, the quarterback has to deal with the present because if he does not deal with that 6′7″ 260-pound linebacker gearing up to come at him at nearly 20 miles (32 km) per hour, he will never get to the future and will never succeed. The quarterback has to deal with the present just to survive.

At the same time, on the other side of the split screen, the quarterback is visualizing the future. He is visualizing where receivers are going to be in about 3.2 seconds, and in his mind, he is working his way back from the future to the present to figure out what he has to do right now to successfully get to that future.

Now, for those of you who don't follow American football, consider a midfielder on a soccer team who wants to send a team member in on a breakaway behind the defenders. She also works in split screen. On one screen, she focuses on the present—on the defender who is coming straight at her. On the other screen, she visualizes where her winger is going to be in about three seconds and works her way back from the future to the present to figure out what she needs to do now to get the ball to that future.

Urban anthropologist and author Jennifer James (1997) calls this mental technique *thinking in the future tense*. Thinking in the future tense requires that you view the present as nothing more than the past of the future. At their core, both quarterbacks and midfielders are futurists—and for being able to use a split screen, they can get paid very well.

THINKING IN THE FUTURE TENSE

In the same way that quarterbacks and midfielders use the split screen to think in future tense, educators also need to be able to effectively use this mindset. This is because one of our many jobs as educators is to make a reasoned extrapolation of what learners will need to live and work in the world of tomorrow based on current trends. Once we have done that, we need to work our way back from the future to the present to determine what we need to do *now* to help our learners successfully prepare for that future.

Although this may seem relatively straightforward, we also acknowledge that, for educators, it is a challenge to project out to the year 2038, just as it is hard to predict the musical groups and political figures in 2038. That's because, given the everyday demands of being an educator, even while we are trying to think in the future tense on one screen, we still must deal with the reality of the here and now on the other screen. We must deal with the demands of getting our learners ready for their next class, day, topic, test, term, education level, or whatever other compliance requirements we have to meet.

At the same time, it is critical to remember that the purpose of education is not, and cannot just be, about attaining short-term goals. Effective education is about identifying and doing the things that are necessary to help our learners prepare for the lives they will live once they complete their schooling (for some ideas, see Chapter 3).

Thinking in future tense—that is, using the split screen—is about finding a balance between the here and now and the future. It's about stepping back from the tyranny of the urgent and considering the bigger picture. It's about where life is heading for our learners and recognizing the critical skills, knowledge, and habits of mind they will need to operate effectively in future environments.

THE BIGGEST CHALLENGES FOR THE FUTURE OF EDUCATION

If we were to ask a group made up of individuals from both inside and outside the current school system to define what the main challenges are with education, we would likely get a wide range of answers and some very strong opinions. They would likely vary from inexplicably vague notions like "not enough technology" or "kids don't listen anymore," to more informed insights that tackle crucial issues like a need for developing critical-thinking skills and problem-solving mindsets in future thinkers and leaders. These more informed insights are aligned with the importance of thinking in the future tense.

Mark Strand (1934–2014), an American poet, proclaimed, "The future is always beginning now" (Strand, 2016, p. i). Education in the new digital landscape is facing more than its fair share of challenges and likely will continue to do so. In times of uncertainty, bordering on fundamental instability, and as we face the relentless challenge of change, it is important to remember that the future is most certainly happening right now.

So, let's look at the future of education and see how we can help both ourselves and our learners prepare for the world of tomorrow, today. In the following sections, we offer some reflective questions or exercises categorized under important themes relevant to the future of education. We do not intend to answer these questions or address these scenarios here; rather, we want them to act as a primer for the next chapter as we focus on education's future. As you reflect on these questions and exercises, think about how you would answer them for your school and your classroom.

Reflection Questions and Exercises to Prompt Thinking About the Future of Learning

Dealing With Change

- How are changing times affecting your school and community, your teaching practices, and your students?
- How can we change teacher preparation programs and professional learning networks so that each helps to develop the types of modern-world learning environments we seek to create for learners?
- How does an organization bring along the change-resistant crowd who is happy with TTWWADI and the status quo?
- How do we start the conversation with our communities about the need to move our schools from where they are to where they need to be?
- How do we help learners prepare today for the kind of living, working, and learning that they will need to survive in 2038?

Determining Modern Skills

- What are the essential 21st century skill sets that are necessary for both educators and learners?
- What are the skills that employers are looking for in the globalized world?
- What are the core skills all high school graduates need to have and be able to do well to be prepared for college, careers, and citizenship?
- Since we cannot teach everything, what are the most important skills and what is the most important knowledge that we should teach?
- What changes do we need in how we train educators, how they work together in schools, and how we supervise and evaluate them to enable them to continuously improve?

Improving Evaluation

- How do we evaluate student knowledge and progress? Does our current way of doing things reflect what students need to know in the 21st century?
- How do we create a better assessment and accountability system that provides the information we need to ensure that all learners are learning essential skills?
- How do we support our educators while at the same time hold them accountable for results?
- What indicators will tell us that we are successful in helping our learners prepare for tomorrow's world?

(Continued)

(Continued)

- What does a high school or college career made up of traditional exam scores tell us about a student's readiness to put knowledge into practice in creative ways?
- How does traditional assessment relate to the kinds of tests our learners will encounter in their lives beyond the classroom?

Developing Better Learning Environments

- Reflect on the nature of schools and learning environments in the 21st century.
- What implications does the shift in our economy have on young people and the ways we design and organize our schools?
- What do good schools, where all learners are mastering the skills that matter most, look like? What can we learn from these schools?
- How can traditional classrooms be transformed into effective learning spaces for all types of learners?
- What challenging environments will learners need to experience to develop the complex abilities they will require for the future?

- Is *school* a physical place, such as a campus or building, or is it the instructional learning process? Why?

Establishing Modern-Day Pedagogy

- Reflect on teaching in the 21st century and how we must change the classroom experience to anticipate students' future needs.
- What new instructional strategies have already been put into place to reach modern-day and future learners? What old strategies can we modify, revise, or move beyond to reach modern-day and future learners?
- If we need people to think differently, solve problems, and be prepared for jobs that don't exist, using technologies that haven't been invented, how can we structure learning experiences with curricula that are outdated before learners access them?
- How can educators use project-based learning in high-tech, low-tech, or no-tech learning environments?
- What strategies must educators use to keep up-to-date on developments in their fields of expertise? What newsletters, online newsgroups, specialty websites, web portals, social media feeds, and other resources exist to help us with this task?

Looking Back, Moving Forward Digital Collection

Extend your knowledge of **how to better prepare learners for education's future** by visiting http://bit.ly/BHFEC5. If you are interested in adding a resource to this collection of curated articles, contact us on Twitter (@ijukes or @RyanLSchaaf).

Chapter Summary

In this chapter, you read about the need to look back to better understand how to move forward. As you reflect on this chapter, make sure you internalize the following key points.

- New individuals, trends, and technologies have superseded the individuals, trends, and technologies of the past; however, we can still observe parallels between the characteristics of schools in 1998 and 2018.

- To effectively prepare students for their futures, educators must use current trends to make a reasoned extrapolation of what skills and attributes learners will need to live and work in the future.

- Thinking in future tense—that is, using split screen—is about finding a balance between the here and now and the future. Educators must consider both short-term and long-term needs for their learners.

Questions to Consider

- In light of the fundamental changes that have taken place in our society in the past twenty-five years, what does it mean to be an educated adult in the 21st century?

- What are the core skills all teachers need to know and be able to do well to adequately prepare our learners for college, careers, and citizenship?

- What are the best ways to know whether learners have mastered the skills that matter most?

6

LEARNING IN
THE YEAR 2038

Let us make our future now, and let us make our dreams tomorrow's reality.

—Malala Yousafzai (MacQuarrie, 2013)

BASED on the content of the past few chapters, the evidence for a change in how we educate students is compelling. The economy has changed, the workplace has changed, society has changed, we have changed, and more important, students, the future of our world, have changed. These are the reasons why we must not put off any longer starting to rethink teaching, learning, and assessment to reflect the modern times in which we live. Maintaining a TTWWADI mindset just won't cut it anymore.

To remain viable in the modern and future world, learners require new skills. The question is, Just what exactly are these new skills? In his best-selling book *The Global Achievement Gap: Why Even Our Best Schools Don't Teach the New Survival Skills Our Children Need—and What We Can Do About It*, world-renowned Harvard University fellow and author Tony Wagner (2010) identifies the following seven survival skills for the 21st century:

1. Critical Thinking and Problem Solving

2. Collaboration Across Networks and Leading by Influence

3. Agility and Adaptability

4. Initiative and Entrepreneurialism

5. Effective Written and Oral Communication

6. Accessing and Analyzing Information

7. Curiosity and Imagination

In much the same manner, in his text *Education 3.0: Seven Steps to Better Schools*, James Lengel (2012) identifies the following six principles of future learning:

1. Students working on problems worth solving

2. Students and teachers collaborating productively

3. Students engaging in self-directed research

4. Students learning how to tell a good story

5. Students employing tools appropriately to the task

6. Students learning to be curious and creative

When you compare Wagner's (2010) and Lengel's (2012) lists, there is significant overlap in the skills they identify, including such areas as problem solving, collaboration, communication, research, and curiosity, all skills that we return to and examine in detail in Chapter 7. They also place emphasis on learning how to effectively use new tools and data.

Based on these identified skill sets, the critical questions that remain are as follows: What will the future of education look like, and how do we get there? How and what should future generations learn? How should education help learners prepare for a global workforce that pits their skills, knowledge, and expertise against equally skilled, lower-paid workers from other countries? Beyond this, how will these same learners compete in a workforce increasingly driven by software, apps, robots, and artificial intelligence?

To address these questions, let's get back into our time machine from Chapter 5 and return once again to the year 2038. This time we're going to do more than ask ourselves largely theoretical questions. This time, let's get inspired by reading Jules Verne, watching Marty McFly at the Enchantment Under the Sea Dance, traveling warp 10 aboard the USS *Enterprise* around a star, or experiencing a quantum leap with Dr. Sam Beckett, and consider a typical day in the life of a student in 2038. With this view of the future in hand, we offer eleven specific predictions for what learning and our schools might look like in the year 2038.

A DAY IN THE LIFE OF ALICE

As the space-time continuum accepts our temporary presence, consider a day in the life of young Alice, a third-grade student at Arcadia Elementary School.

Alice's teacher, Ms. Crabtree, has provided her class with a series of problem-based learning challenges associated with the theme *Saving the World From Environmental Pollution*. Ms. Crabtree has tasked Alice's group, which consists of herself, Nolan, and a few other students, with decreasing the amount of trash the school generates. Alice's group is one of fifteen teams whom Ms. Crabtree has challenged to find solutions to various environmental issues. Today is the day when they report their progress to their class and teachers.

As we review Alice's day, also try to uncover evidence of the crucial skills Wagner (2010), Lengel (2012), and others have identified as being essential to survive and thrive in the future.

7:25 a.m.	Alice wakes up rubbing her eyes. Last night, she stayed up late to conduct research on environmental pollution and ways to decrease the harm this causes our world.	Students engage in self-directed research
	Solving this problem is a passion for Alice, one that she is tirelessly working on. She asks her ever-present, always-connected personal digital assistant, EVA, if she has any messages. The first is a message from her teammate Nolan asking if she received data from the school custodian about the amount of trash the school produced in the past fourteen days. The second message is an email from Dr. Amanda Avery, a world-renowned ecologist, presently working in Antarctica on combating global pollution, confirming her video conference for 3 p.m.	Collaboration Across Networks and Leading by Influence
8:10 a.m.	Alice finishes up her breakfast and takes a few minutes to watch her favorite show courtesy of her high-speed, cloud-based web server that streams any media format within a matter of milliseconds. She asks EVA to review her schedule and to email each of her teammates to remind them to bring all the resources they need for "the big day."	
8:30 a.m.	Alice asks EVA to verify that all her project files are synched to her iDEA Pad—an all-in-one device that contains the functionality of a digital tablet, smartphone, and digital camera, complete with a built-in holographic 3-D projector to display images, video, data, and a visual interface with a mobile version of EVA. She places her iDEA Pad into her backpack along with her lunch and walks the five minutes to school.	
8:40 a.m.	As Alice enters the building, EVA interfaces with the school's network, indicating that she is present and that she will not need to buy lunch today. Alice briefly reports to her mentor-teacher, Ms. Crabtree, before heading to meet Nolan and the rest of her group in the Learning Lab.	
8:45 a.m.	As she enters the lab, Nolan asks, "Did Mr. Nelson provide you with the data?" Alice pulls out her iDEA Pad and shows the group the results. "Wow, look at the decline in the volume of trash over the past fourteen days. Our action plan to decrease the garbage the school produces worked," says Nolan.	Collaboration Across Networks and Leading by Influence
9 a.m.	Alice attends the morning meeting with the rest of her study group together with twenty learners who Ms. Crabtree organized into five teams. Each of the teams is exploring a different aspect of the *Saving the World* theme. The learning space, complete with comfortable, adaptable furniture, has a flexible floor plan that allows the teams to easily transition for independent, group, or whole-class activities.	
	Ms. Crabtree meets with each group for ten minutes to get a status update and offer guidance for their work for the day. During this time, Alice's group shares its findings, while Ms. Crabtree offers advice and suggestions, and points the students toward resources. When Ms. Crabtree leaves, the group uses its research skills to find the elements of a line graph in the data the students collected, identify trusted sources, and create a detailed and visually appealing graph.	Students and teachers collaborate productively Accessing and Analyzing Information, and Students engage in self-directed research
10 a.m.	Alice heads to the school's Maker Learning Lab to continue her work on designing wind turbine blades that will	Students work on problems worth solving

generate clean power for their community. The learning lab is equipped with 3-D printers, so after students develop their turbine blades, they can test the prototypes by comparing them to a working model of a wind turbine.

> Students employ tools appropriately to the task

During the hour, Alice and EVA design and test four prototype blades on her iDEA Pad. Mr. Alonso, her Maker Learning Lab facilitator, uses probing questions to provide Alice with constructive feedback and guidance for future blade designs. Some of his questions include, What is causing the turbine blades to increase in rotational speed? Does the size of the turbine blade impact the amount of electricity generated? and How does the speed of the wind impact the speed of the blades? He asks her to include data to support her observations.

> Students and teachers collaborate productively

11:15 a.m. Alice makes her way to a large learning commons to participate in a literacy class. Here, students select from a collection of tens of thousands of digital books associated with environmental sciences. Alice reads two challenging texts about the Amazon rain forest. She is particularly interested in the biodiversity that exists within a square acre of forest. Alice uses her iDEA Pad to create a 3-D hologram of a small area of the Amazon rain forest, complete with insects and animals flying or scurrying through the virtual diorama. Adrian and Lisa, two of her classmates who are particularly interested in her hologram, ask questions about flora and fauna on the rain forest floor and suggest adding a small stream to better reflect the fact that the Amazon contains many bodies of water.

> Students learn to be curious, creative, and imaginative

> Students employ tools appropriately to the task

12:15 p.m. Alice enjoys her lunch in the café as she and her friends discuss their progress in the Maker Learning Lab, and each of them shares a little information about his or her different group projects. One student, Raul, is creating a compost heap for the school and exploring the possibility of placing some additional heaps in local communities to decrease trash and to create free fertilizer for the neighborhood. Another student, Michael, discusses a story he found while researching a solution for cleaning trash from bodies of water. He read an article about Boyan Slat and his incredible creation called the Ocean Cleanup Array, which he designed to clear all plastic bottles out of the ocean. Michael is brainstorming ideas for making a smaller version to clean the local streams in the area. Finally, Alice's best friend, Michelle, is working on a community cleanup fun run, where volunteers will participate in a 5K while simultaneously picking up trash.

> Critical Thinking and Problem Solving

> Initiative and Entrepreneurialism

12:45 p.m. Alice goes outside for recess for some physical activity. She participates in the kinds of physical activities any young girl would wish to do to decompress after an engaging but cognitively taxing morning. During a previous instructional theme called *Use Your Words*, Alice's team made a compelling presentation to the school principal suggesting that she increase recess by an additional ten minutes a day. Students now receive forty-five minutes a day, with two additional recess times spread throughout the week.

> Students work on problems worth solving, Agility and Adaptability

1:30 p.m.	Alice's group meets to finalize the work it completed during the collaborative project. The students decide to provide a presentation to the other learners as well as Dr. Avery in Antarctica. Nolan starts the presentation by noting that their school previously produced more than five hundred pounds of trash per day. They then share the research about ways to reduce the accumulation of trash, as well as how they worked with Mr. Nelson to inform the student body of the methods the school can employ to decrease the amount of trash it generates. Over the course of two weeks, their efforts reduced the amount of trash the school produced from 500 pounds to 235 pounds—a 47 percent reduction!

Accessing and Analyzing Information

3 p.m.	Ms. Crabtree asks the class to virtually welcome Dr. Avery as she shares some of the work she has been conducting in Antarctica to study the effects of environmental pollution. For more than fifteen minutes, she provides an overview of her work. Alice and her group then deliver an impassioned presentation about their trash reduction study. They share how they used Dr. Avery's work to implement a plan at their school that was a great success. For twenty minutes, Dr. Avery, Ms. Crabtree, and the rest of the class listen and ask questions based on the content of their presentation. It's apparent the group performed exceptionally well. At the end of the presentation, Ms. Crabtree asks each group member to write a personal reflection on the project and the process, as well as for students to place their materials in their student portfolios.

Students learn how to tell a good story, and Effective Written and Oral Communication

3:45 p.m.	Alice and her team listen attentively to another group that provides a presentation on protecting endangered species. The group presenting is not as far along as Alice's team, so the class offers them advice on how to proceed with their research. After working on her diorama, Alice suggests the other group use a similar visual model to demonstrate how everything is connected in the food web by showing what happens when animals begin to disappear from the web. The group making the presentation thanks the others for the feedback.

Collaboration

4 p.m.	Alice arrives home and has a snack. She asks EVA to load and start her favorite music playlist and to recite the book she has been reading as she eats. She completes her homework and reviews the key components she explored during the day.
4:30 p.m.	EVA shares some of the twenty-three messages Alice received throughout the day. A few were video clips from her parents; others were friends asking about some playdates; and a few were compliments on her presentation, including one email from a student in Singapore who was interested in her work on trash reduction.
5 p.m.	Alice eats dinner in a hurry so she can play with her friends.
6:30 p.m.	Alice plays a video game called *Synapse* with her family. The game has players race around a network of tunnels to get the fastest times. The game also helps real doctors map the neural pathways of patients suffering from dementia. The 1.5 billion players have been able to help reconstruct the brains of over twenty patients.
7:30 p.m.	Alice places EVA into power-down recharge mode and begins to read a paperback book before she gets ready for bed.
8:30 p.m.	Alice drifts away to sleep. Her day is over.

Alice's day was filled with exciting, relevant, fulfilling, and active learning experiences. More than that, however, it represented a learning model that supports Wagner's (2010), Lengel's (2012), and others' visions about what the future of education must look like if we are going to help learners prepare themselves for the many challenges that await them once they leave school. These are schools that transform themselves from traditional content distributors to cultivators of modern and future-day skills.

ELEVEN PREDICTIONS OF LEARNING IN THE YEAR 2038

Emerging trends suggest that learning will look much different in the year 2038 (McCain, Jukes, & Crockett, 2010). Based on the timeline we just envisioned, we developed eleven predictions about what we believe learning will look like circa 2038, together with some approaches we believe educators and school leaders can employ to prepare their schools and learners for that very future.

11 Predictions About Learning in 2038

1. Learning will be just in time.

2. Learning will happen anytime, anyplace, in both virtual and physical spaces.

3. Learning will be lifelong.

4. Learning will be personalized, learner-centered, and nonlinear.

5. Learning will be whole-minded.

6. Learning will be real-world.

7. Learning will be discovery-based.

8. Learning will be focused on processing multimedia information.

9. Learning will be collaborative.

10. Learning will be assisted by thinking machines, smart agents, and big data.

11. Learning and evaluation will be holistic.

In the following sections, we examine each of these predictions in detail.

PREDICTION #1: LEARNING WILL BE JUST IN TIME

In Chapter 4, we introduced the concepts of just-in-case learning and just-in-time learning. We are rapidly entering an era that will demand just-in-time learning, which stands in dramatic contrast to the just-in-case model many schools currently use—just in case the content is on the exam, just in case we might need to use this content in our careers, or just in case this content might be important. One of the main reasons schools must prepare students for a world that demands lifelong learning is that the incredible amount of information bombarding us grows daily. "By 2020, information will be doubling every 20 minutes—this means there will be eight times as much information at the end of a 60-minute class than there was at the beginning" (Rankin, 2011).

Learning on a need-to-know basis parallels an evolution in the business world that began during the early 1980s. At that time, there was a fundamental shift in the manufacturing of products to something called *just-in-time delivery* (Hindle, 2009). Companies no longer stockpile huge warehouses full of inventory; rather, they only begin to order the materials they need when a customer orders a product from them.

Because we live in a time of increasingly disposable information, much of learning must shift to just-in-time learning, where students access information and conceptual material only when they are necessary. For example, many businesses periodically pull workers away from their regular duties to learn new techniques, methods, and skills that they need to continue performing well at their jobs.

As we discussed throughout Chapter 3, knowledge and skills students acquire by age twenty are obsolete by age forty, if not before. If this trend continues, we project that 2018's learners will have to replace almost their entire body of knowledge several times during their working lives. As a result, increasingly we live in a world where people must constantly manage their careers, figuring out what they need to do next if they are going to keep themselves relevant and employed in an ever-changing economy. Market forces will compel schools to embrace the just-in-time mindset.

#1 Just-in-Time Resources

1. **YouTube.** Learners find YouTube far more engaging than reading and writing. Did you know that most of the videos are about learning something? (Donchev, 2017). As a platform that embodies the just-in-time ethos of the future, YouTube has become one of the most powerful tools for educators and learners alike. Learners go to YouTube to discover a new strategy to win a video game, to find out how to fix a bicycle chain, or just for the fun of it. They use YouTube to share their insights and experiences to help others solve problems or learn new skills. Traditional instruction has a really hard time competing with this kind of always-on, visual learning.

2. **Khan Academy.** Khan Academy is another excellent resource that provides an extensive catalog for helping learners learn just about anything. Khan Academy offers practice activities, instructional videos, and a personalized learning dashboard that enables learners to work anytime, anyplace, at any pace, both inside and outside school. Mathematics, history, science, economics, and computer programming are just a few of the many subjects available for free.

3. **Online searches.** What's the capital of Peru? What's the distance between Mars and Earth? Why does the ocean have tides? These are just a few of the countless questions educators are bombarded with each day. When teachers answer their learners' questions, it takes the power away from learners and places the responsibility to provide the answers directly on the shoulders of the teachers. The hardest-working person in the classroom should never be the teacher—it

should always be the learners. You will read those words from us again before you are done with this book, because it is imperative that educators help students learn to ask their own questions and find their own answers using the many powerful tools and resources at their disposal. To do this, learners must not only feel comfortable searching Google, Wikipedia, books, and other digital and nondigital sources to answer higher-order thinking questions without an educator intervening—they must also have the essential skills needed to effectively navigate massive amounts of information and discern the difference between fact and fiction.

PREDICTION #2: LEARNING WILL HAPPEN ANYTIME, ANYPLACE, IN BOTH VIRTUAL AND PHYSICAL SPACES

For more than 150 years, society expected learners to come to the school (in a physical sense). This is not necessarily the way it will always be, which may come as a real shock to many of us who have spent most of our lives either teaching or learning in a classroom. The development of global digital networks has fundamentally revolutionized the concept of travel. Almost everyone has access, anytime and anywhere, to anyone and anything using personal, pocket-sized, wireless devices.

Schools must take advantage of the fact that an overwhelming majority of forms of information and communication are in digital formats. With global digital networks rapidly blanketing the entire planet and pocket-sized mobile devices continuing to proliferate, schools can embrace an extensive and versatile array of digital tools, software, apps, and resources that make it possible to create personal virtual learning environments. These environments allow participants to learn from anyone, anywhere, anytime, and at any pace.

As a result, learning in the future will not need to be confined to a specific location or single source. Learners will remain in constant contact with their teacher and classmates whenever and wherever in the world they are. As a result, learning can happen at home, on the job, in the community, or wherever the learner is at that moment.

#2 Anyplace, Anytime Learning Resources

1. **Video conferencing.** Digital devices make it easy for people to connect virtually. Digital tools such as Slack, Skype, and Google Hangouts allow real-time text communication and video conferencing to occur in a wide variety of forms: student-to-student, student-to-group, group-to-group, class-to-teacher, class-to-class, and class-to-expert are just a few of the many ways learners and educators can connect to one another using digital tools.

2. **Learning management systems.** Many instructional organizations use learning management systems or student information systems that provide a range of educational support services such as administration, documentation,

(Continued)

(Continued)

tracking, and reporting and delivery of educational courses or training programs.

3. **Podcasts.** People can also learn informally while online. Downloading and listening to podcasts allows learners to take their studies and passions with them, all stored in their digital, second, external brain otherwise known as a smartphone. An excellent example of this phenomenon is the *Serial* (n.d.) podcast, which, as of February 2016, more than eighty million listeners had downloaded, capturing global interest.

4. **Online classes.** New opportunities are available for learners through online course catalogs hosted at sources such as Woz U, Udemy, Coursera, iTunes U, and others. Learners can explore thermodynamics, computer programming, photography, cooking, theoretical physics, creative writing, and thousands of other courses and subjects. Learning no longer needs to occur only within the traditional two-by-four-by-six classroom—no more need for the traditional two covers of a book, four walls of a classroom, or six periods a day.

PREDICTION #3: LEARNING WILL BE LIFELONG

In the 21st century, schools must prepare students for the reality that learning must be a lifelong process. Trend analysis we established in Chapter 3 ("Careers in the New Global Economy") suggests that our children can anticipate they will have ten to seventeen or more distinct careers in their working lifetimes. This is not different jobs working for the same company or in the same industry but *distinct* careers (Doyle, 2017).

Schools must prepare students for a future in which job changes are a recurring fact of life. This comment is borne out of data from the U.S. Bureau of Labor Statistics (2017) that state that one out of two workers has been working for his or her current company for less than one year and that two out of three have been working for the same company for less than five years. Part of preparing students for this future means embracing and making students aware of the many resources they have to further their own learning, not just while they are in their schooling years but for after they enter the working world.

#3 Lifelong Learning Resources

With the emergence of the new digital landscape, there has never been the level of access to both formal and informal learning opportunities as there is today. Resources such as community colleges, learning annexes, libraries, and other continuing education programs have been available for decades. They traditionally offer a broad range of formal education and career training for individuals who want to increase their salaries, earn promotions, or perform career switches.

However, the disruptive times we live in have created new opportunities for lifelong, just-in-time learning.

1. **Online resources and classes.** We have already discussed that with services like YouTube, Woz U, and Coursera, learning can happen at any time and in any place. Massive open online courses allow large numbers of people to inexpensively attend a range of diverse classes virtually from the comfort of their living rooms on their own

schedule. There are also literally thousands of online tools that allow individuals to curate and share knowledge.

2. **Social media.** The digital generations use Snapchat, Instagram, Twitter, YouTube, reddit, and Tumblr to communicate, collaborate, and share ideas in an ever-expanding universe of knowledge. Educators have also embraced social media using tools such as Twitter and Pinterest to create personal and professional learning networks to share ideas and resources.

3. **Initiative.** Being an educator can be a formidable task. Professional challenges never entirely disappear. The problem is that these challenges often do not occur at convenient times, such as during a personal training or professional development session. Regardless of our age or proximity to retirement, we must all be prepared to learn outside of traditional educational channels. Everyone from workers to parents to learners—even educators—must never stop learning—and schools cannot be the only venue for individuals to develop new skills and acquire new knowledge. By the time they have completed their formal education, students must be self-motivated to take courses, read books, ask colleagues for advice, network with others, seek out the latest trends, and keep themselves up-to-date through their own initiative.

PREDICTION #4: LEARNING WILL BE PERSONALIZED, LEARNER-CENTERED, AND NONLINEAR

The traditional educational mindset involves a cookie-cutter curriculum, which leads to a one-size-fits-all mentality for learning. This approach operates on the assumption that all learners can learn the same material, in the same way, and in the same time frames.

Unfortunately, this strategy does not work for many people. In the United States alone, and as we briefly mentioned in Chapter 3 (The Dropout Problem), the dropout rate for high school learners continues to be substantial. Even though it has improved since 2015, having nearly 20 percent of learners leaving schools before completion is entirely unacceptable (Camera, 2015). Although it may be easiest to assume that there must be something wrong with the dropouts who have left the school system, a 2014 study concludes that the two primary reasons learners drop out are that the student is failing (27.6 percent) and that school was boring (25.9 percent) (Gould & Weller, 2015).

William Butler Yeats stated that "education is not the filling of a pail, but the lighting of a fire" (as cited in Moore, 2010). An educator's job is to create a roaring blaze of passion for learning that sustains itself not just for a day or a week or a month but for a lifetime. Learning can no longer be about controlling learners—it must be about empowering them to explore their creativity, discover their passions, and help prepare themselves for the world that awaits them once they leave school.

Personal digital devices also break the time barrier for learning because learning no longer needs to be over when the bell has rung, at the end of a period, or the end of the school day. In the same way, school districts no longer need to predicate the school day and school year on the traditional 180 days a year, five and a half hours a day. Using new technologies, learning can be personalized. This kind of learning provides the opportunity to offer a diverse range of educational programs, learning experiences, instructional approaches, and academic support strategies designed to meet the distinct learning needs and interests of individual students (The Glossary of Education Reform, 2015). Learners can access learning materials anytime and anyplace, twenty-four hours a day, 365 days a year. This has enormous implications, because it means that need and interest can drive learning rather than a clock, calendar, or curriculum.

#4 Personalized Learning Resources

1. **BYOD.** The customization and personalization of learning begins with the everyday tools learners have at their disposal. A popular trend in schools is Bring Your Own Device (BYOD) initiatives. This refers to the practice of learners bringing their laptops, tablets, smartphones, or other mobile devices with them to the learning environment. This approach helps institutions save money, while simultaneously boosting learner productivity, because they are already comfortable using their own devices. More important, BYOD initiatives help educators move the primary focus away from learning new software to an emphasis on pedagogy. In other words, the focus is on the task and not the tool.

2. **Learning centers.** Learning centers are another approach that promotes student agency, because they offer the opportunity for learners to experience a personal level of control, autonomy, and power within their learning environments. When implementing learning centers, teachers thoughtfully place instructional activities throughout the learning space together with the essential tools and materials learners can use to explore and review new concepts. This approach helps decentralize learning and provides learners with the opportunity to select the centers they most need to experience. These activities are all built into dynamic learning environments where teachers are free to move throughout the learning space, engaging with learners on an individualized basis.

3. **Genius hour.** Learning experiences such as *genius hour* (otherwise known as *20% Time, 20Time, 20-Time,* and *20 percent time*) allow learners to explore a range of subjects, topics, and personal areas of interest using approximately 20 percent of allotted instructional time. Companies such as Google, 3M, and Apple (Baldwin, 2012; Mogg,

2012) have found great success permitting their employees to spend 20 percent of their working time developing personal passion projects. Whereas in a traditional classroom, it is common practice for learners to lack any personal control of their learning environments, even though having learners explore their passions in a learning context allows them to become intrinsically motivated to learn because they have personal ownership of the learning. Just as Apple's concept of a Genius Bar offers in-store technical support for customers, in an educational context, a genius hour involves learners sharing their specialized knowledge and expertise in a range of academic and nonacademic subjects with their peers.

4. **Universal Design for Learning.** Still another idea for diversifying instructional approaches involves using the Universal Design for Learning framework. The framework (see Figure 6.1), based on scientific research about how humans learn and how to optimize teaching and learning, provides principles for curriculum development that give individuals greater opportunity to learn. It provides flexible goals, methods, materials, and assessments that empower educators to meet the varied needs of their learners (Center for Applied Special Technology, 2011).

5. **Learners as prosumers.** Learners must share their voices when they create and publish multimedia products. Digital generations spend countless hours of their time both consuming and producing multimedia content, to the point where they transform from multimedia consumers to multimedia prosumers (simultaneous consumers and producers) (Jukes et al., 2015). Multimedia prosumers are people who can demonstrate their excitement and share their passions, insights, and performances with authentic audiences in the connected world.

FIGURE 6.1

Universal Design for Learning guidelines

The Universal Design for Learning Guidelines

CAST | Until learning has no limits

Provide multiple means of **Engagement**	Provide multiple means of **Representation**	Provide multiple means of **Action & Expression**
Affective Networks The "WHY" of Learning	Recognition Networks The "WHAT" of Learning	Strategic Networks The "HOW" of Learning

Access

Provide options for
Recruiting Interest (7)
- Optimize individual choice and autonomy (7.1)
- Optimize relevance, value, and authenticity (7.2)
- Minimize threats and distractions (7.3)

Provide options for
Perception (1)
- Offer ways of customizing the display of information (1.1)
- Offer alternatives for auditory information (1.2)
- Offer alternatives for visual information (1.3)

Provide options for
Physical Action (4)
- Vary the methods for response and navigation (4.1)
- Optimize access to tools and assistive technologies (4.2)

Build

Provide options for
Sustaining Effort & Persistence (8)
- Heighten salience of goals and objectives (8.1)
- Vary demands and resources to optimize challenge (8.2)
- Foster collaboration and community (8.3)
- Increase mastery-oriented feedback (8.4)

Provide options for
Language & Symbols (2)
- Clarify vocabulary and symbols (2.1)
- Clarify syntax and structure (2.2)
- Support decoding of text, mathematical notation, and symbols (2.3)
- Promote understanding across languages (2.4)
- Illustrate through multiple media (2.5)

Provide options for
Expression & Communication (5)
- Use multiple media for communication (5.1)
- Use multiple tools for construction and composition (5.2)
- Build fluencies with graduated levels of support for practice and performance (5.3)

Internalize

Provide options for
Self Regulation (9)
- Promote expectations and beliefs that optimize motivation (9.1)
- Facilitate personal coping skills and strategies (9.2)
- Develop self-assessment and reflection (9.3)

Provide options for
Comprehension (6)
- Activate or supply background knowledge (3.1)
- Highlight patterns, critical features, big ideas, and relationships (3.2)
- Guide information processing and visualization (3.3)
- Maximize transfer and generalization (3.4)

Provide options for
Executive Functions (6)
- Guide appropriate goal-setting (6.1)
- Support planning and strategy development (6.2)
- Facilitate managing information and resources (6.3)
- Enhance capacity for monitoring progress (6.4)

Goal

Expert learners who are...

Purposeful & Motivated	Resourceful & Knowledgeable	Strategic & Goal-Directed

udlguidelines.cast.org | © CAST, Inc. 2018 | CAST (2018). Universal design for learning guidelines version 2.2 [graphic organizer]. Wakefield, MA: Author.

PREDICTION #5: LEARNING WILL BE WHOLE-MINDED

Modern science has helped humans better understand some of the mysteries associated with the brain. Although a great deal of the brain's capabilities continues to puzzle scientists, we do have a growing understanding of how the brain functions and learns.

Contrary to traditional assumptions that the brain is stable from about three years of age onward, we now understand that the digital generations' brains are

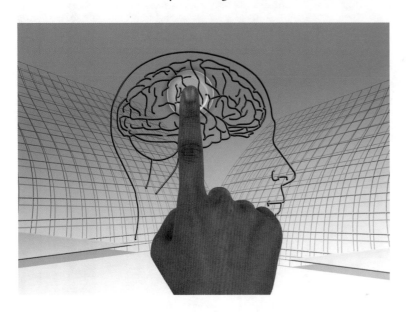

constantly creating new thinking patterns throughout their lives, which affects the way they interact with the world (Jukes, McCain, & Crockett, 2010). We introduced this phenomenon at the start of this chapter as neuroplasticity—the human brain's ability to reorganize its neural structure or even produce large-scale change such as cortical remapping on an ongoing basis.

In the digital age, information in many media formats constantly bombards the human brain. This digital bombardment compels individuals to develop a rapidly changing set of physical and mental skills.

Schools can take advantage of this knowledge to provide resources best suited to the developing brains of their students.

#5 Whole-Minded Learning Resources

1. **Provide a broad range of learning experiences.** Learners require a broad range of experiences that engage their cognitive potential and inspire their imaginations. This is hard to do in classrooms that regularly engage in a worksheet culture. Instead, educators must plan experiences and activities that stimulate different parts of students' brains.

2. **Get students moving.** Incorporate movement and exercise into the classroom. From an evolutionary standpoint, humans are biologically programmed to walk up to twenty miles a day (Medina, 2008). Exercise increases the production of

neurochemicals that increase brain cell repair, improves memory, lengthens attention spans, boosts decision-making skills, prompts growth of new blood cells and vessels, and improves multitasking abilities (Heid, 2011).

Simple tasks and exercises such as jumping jacks, gallery walks, nature walks, musical chairs, and bouncing or playing catch with a ball are just a few examples of incorporating physical activities. There are numerous ways for educators to incorporate movement. Some include creating multiple workstations and learning centers, and making frequent transitions throughout the instructional day. There is also a fun online service called GoNoodle, which incorporates movement and brain breaks for students. GoNoodle provides hundreds of videos that get kids running, jumping, dancing, stretching, and practicing mindful moments.

3. **Incorporate music.** Teresa Lesiuk, a professor in music therapy at the University of Miami, finds that "those who listened to music completed their tasks more quickly and came up with better ideas than those who didn't because the music improved their mood" (Padnani, 2012). Music can be a powerful incentive for learners during work time. It can be used as a reward for beginning and maintaining workflow or demonstrating positive behavior. Incorporating music into the classroom also has an impact on the human brain and productivity. Because melodious sounds encourage the release of dopamine in the reward area of the brain, playing music during a classroom activity can be used as a powerful incentive. The music provides learners with the instant gratification found in dopamine release, but there is also the strong possibility that learners will improve long-term work habits if the music is linked to their classroom experiences.

4. **Establish makerspaces.** The maker movement is sprouting a vibrant culture of people who learn by doing. They tinker with materials and tools to create new products, explore new concepts, and develop new skills. The uncertain future and a precarious economy will require the digital generations to constantly solve new problems in new ways. To do so, they must cultivate new skills such as fabrication, coding, creativity, design, and research (Martinez & Stager, 2013). The aspects and practices present in tinkering will help cultivate these essential future skills.

5. **Encourage good sleep habits.** Educators can also optimize learning experiences for their learners. Researchers at Boston College found that "the United States had the highest number of sleep-deprived learners, with 73% of 9 and 10-year-olds and 80% of 13 and 14-year-olds identified by their teachers as being adversely affected" (Coughlan, 2013). A lack of sleep drastically decreases cognitive performance (Jensen, 2008). Both educators and parents must instill the need for learners to get enough sleep.

6. **Optimize the design of the learning environment.** Learning institutions must provide environments that are comfortable and engaging for learners. Indirect or diverse lighting sources, proper ventilation, vibrant wall color, and relevant visual displays, together with a lack of allergens, are essential for student engagement. Learners also may prefer sitting on stability balls instead of hard, plastic chairs, standing as they work (standing desks), or stretching out on the floor to complete their task. Schools should maintain classroom temperatures between 68 and 72°F (20–22°C), as this is the ideal temperature for biological and cognitive functioning (Jensen, 2008).

PREDICTION #6: LEARNING WILL BE REAL-WORLD

Academic success in the industrial age was based on a student's ability to memorize large amounts of unrelated content. Educators and employers highly regarded and rewarded people who could be obsequious and regurgitate large amounts of information on demand. However, this intellectual and informational regurgitation does not, by itself, adequately prepare a person for the information age and communication age in which we live. The days when educators could stuff into students' brains all the information they needed are long gone.

It is clear to us that students still need to learn content, but future careers will place much less emphasis on the amount of material they must memorize and far more emphasis on making connections, thinking through issues, and solving problems focused on real-world scenarios and applications.

There is absolutely a place for rote memorization, but the world will place much more value on a student's ability to not only process information but also apply what he or she learned within the context of real-world, real-time problems and challenges that promote the transfer of learning to new situations.

In the 21st century, information has an increasingly short shelf life and quickly becomes disposable. This implies that content specialization must give way to more general knowledge. In other words, as we shift from rote learning to more significant learning, we will witness a parallel shift from specialists to generalists who also have the effective analytical processing skills needed to deal with continuously transient information. While there will always be a place for specialists in fields such as medicine, law, and the sciences, a survey of 2,000 white-collar professionals by recruiter PageGroup found that workers' specialist skills are often being diluted within just two years of them entering a new job (HRreview, 2013). This means that our success in the future will rely not only on what we can remember but also on what we can perceive about the information we are working with, how to transform information into knowledge, how to apply this knowledge to real-world conditions, and our ability to continue learning throughout our lives.

#6 Real-World Resources

1. **Integration of the outside world into the classroom.** This will provide exciting opportunities for learners and schools and the communities they serve. Educators have long considered field trips a staple in education. Field trips allow learners to venture outside of the school building and experience learning in the biggest classroom of all—the global classroom. Local farms, museums, fire stations, and community tours are just a few of the many local trips educators often plan for their learners.

2. **Community projects.** Community projects are work done by individuals or groups for the benefit of others. This volunteer work is often undertaken in close proximity to your neighborhood, so that the local community gains the benefits of the project. Community projects are undertaken for the benefit of a wide variety of groups from children, to seniors, to people with disabilities, even animals and the environment.

3. **Scenario-based learning.** Scenario-based learning (SBL) uses interactive scenarios to support active learning strategies. SBL involves learners working their way through a story line based upon a problem to solve. SBL is an ideal method of instruction because it allows learners

to acquire and apply content knowledge in a real-world manner. Consider the following example of how educators can apply academic content to a real-world scenario that involves coordinated planes.

Many of the coral reefs of the world are rapidly disappearing due to natural and human causes. To prevent the continued erosion of the coral reefs, humans have begun to sink decommissioned naval boats to start new artificial reefs. The hulls of the ships provide a strong foundation for coral to colonize.

In this example, the teacher informs students that the local science center is sponsoring a competition for student groups to become reef designers. Each student group must identify offshore locations for new artificial reefs, then use their knowledge of coordinated planes to locate and record ideal sites for these reefs. The designers must also use coordinated planes to identify and map the locations of existing sites to avoid jeopardizing marine life.

The teacher then informs students that their challenge is to safely lower the ships to the bottom of the ocean to begin the life cycle of the reef. The student groups must prepare a report summarizing the new reef locations, the safety

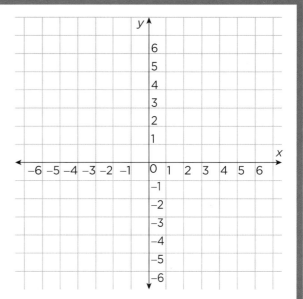

measures used to protect the environment, and the benefits the reef will produce for that area.

Real-world examples, like this one, help students apply their academic learning in ways that also prepare them to face the sorts of challenges they will experience in the professional world.

PREDICTION #7: LEARNING WILL BE DISCOVERY-BASED

The traditional approach to instruction is that teaching means telling things to learners. Also, as learners progress through the school system, the courses teachers provide contain an increasing amount of content they must cover for students to complete the course. When you combine these two factors, it is easy to see why there is an increase in the use of lecture-style instruction as learners move through the school system. If teachers have a great deal of material to cover in a course, and they have to make sure they get through it all, this triggers a natural impulse to begin telling learners what they need to know. As far back as Aristotle (and probably further back than that), teaching has involved teachers passing on their knowledge and wisdom by sharing with their students what they have learned.

As our fellow educator and colleague Ted McCain (2005) states, for many educators, "teaching as telling, learning as listening" has become the default method for instruction. By the time someone becomes a teacher, his or her training has exposed him or her to a great deal of the teaching-as-telling, learning-as-listening approach. This training has unconsciously indoctrinated him or her with the long-established idea that, as learners move through the system, teachers must place more emphasis on teaching as telling and learning as listening.

The problem is that research demonstrates this approach is not the most effective way to teach. In fact, this approach reflects little of what we have come to understand about thinking and learning over the past 150 years, and more important, it is not reflective of education's future. It is important to see that this style of teaching falls into the lowest category of cognitive processing (Medina, 2008).

One of the primary reasons for the lack of effectiveness of the teaching-as-telling, learning-as-listening approach is that learners do not have an active role to play in their learning. Many teachers we work with argue that by updating their teaching to include photos, recordings, colorful websites, PowerPoint slides, movies, and YouTube videos, they can enhance learning experiences in their classrooms. While doing this is laudable, we must note that augmenting the teaching-as-talking approach to include multimedia presentations does not in and of itself help learners reach the higher levels of thinking and learning that are increasingly necessary to operate in the modern world. This teacher-centered approach mostly continues to focus on learners maintaining their roles as passive receivers of information in the learning process rather than being active participants in their own learning.

> This teacher-centered approach mostly continues to focus on learners maintaining their roles as passive receivers of information in the learning process rather than being active participants in their own learning.

Digital generations have grown up with access to highly interactive, hyperlinked, multimedia, online digital environments where they control both the path and the pace of their movement through information. Such environments are in complete contrast with classroom environments where the teacher talks and expects learners to listen, rather than discover knowledge for themselves. Being told what is going to happen in advance robs you of the experience of finding this out for yourself. It removes the elements of wonder and surprise.

Discovery generates the interest that is critical to learning. Richard Saul Wurman (1989) explains it as follows: "Learning can be seen as the acquisition of information, but before it can take place, there must be interest; interest precedes learning. In order to acquire and remember new knowledge, it must stimulate your curiosity in some way" (p. 20).

iStock.com/SteveDebenport

Wurman (1989) goes on to say that trying to learn content without any interest or context to the learner is like having only one side of a piece of Velcro—it just doesn't stick. Our job as teachers is to create the other side of the Velcro—creating interest in the minds of our learners—so the information in our courses sticks in their minds. We believe that this, bar none, is the most important role educators have.

This does not mean that we must stop telling learners things altogether. Telling will always have its place in teaching. But to counterbalance the telling learners receive, we must shift at least some of our instruction to include discovery learning. Discovery is an incredible journey for a young mind. Even if the material is as old as the hills, if it is a new experience for the learner, it has the potential to bring interest and excitement to any learning experience.

#7 Discovery Learning Resources

1. **Acting It Out** is an interactive way for learners to discover a valuable connection to content while simultaneously engaging in active learning. Educators draft a short play, skit, or performance for the learners to act. As the scenario plays out among the actors and observers, they make new discoveries. Why did the man hear the heartbeat in "The Tell-Tale Heart" (Poe, 1843/1982)? Why did Brutus assassinate Caesar? How did four people get across a river in a canoe that only had room for two passengers? Acting It Out is a fun, engaging, and discovery-rich strategy that requires learners to express themselves both verbally and physically at any age in any subject area.

2. **WebQuests.** WebQuests are an inquiry-oriented lesson format in which most or all of the information that learners work with comes from the web. Bernie Dodge (1995) developed this model in the mid-1990s at San Diego State University. A WebQuest is composed of the following six steps.

   1. **Introduction:** The introduction sets the stage, entices learners, and relates the experience to the overall unit or theme. WebQuest introductions should motivate learners to participate. Since WebQuests are inquiry based, they revolve around the essential or guiding question asked in this section.

   2. **Task:** Tasks tell the learners what they are doing. In this section, learners discover what they will be working on and delivering at the end of the WebQuest. The task must clearly define what the expectations are for the learners.

   3. **Process:** The process tells the learners how they will complete the task. This section outlines sequential, detailed, step-by-step instructions for completing the task.

   4. **Resources:** Resources provide the instructional materials, hyperlinks, and documents for the task.

   5. **Evaluation:** The evaluation section identifies how the educator will evaluate the task and end product. This section usually comes with a checklist or rubric.

   6. **Conclusion:** The conclusion asks learners to deliver their end product. Both teachers and learners summarize what they accomplished or learned by completing this activity or lesson as well as return to an essential or guiding question they can answer and reflect upon.

(Continued)

(Continued)

The following are several resources to explore for finding or creating WebQuests.

- WebQuest.org (http://webquest.org)
- Teachnology (www.teach-nology.com/teachers/lesson_plans/computing/web_quests)
- Zunal (http://zunal.com)
- QuickBase (www.quickbase.com/articles/the-complete-guide-to-creating-web-quests)

3. **Mystery Skype**. Mystery Skype is an educational game that connects two classrooms situated in different parts of the world. While the educators know where (and who) they're calling, the students do not. The goal of Mystery Skype is to locate the other class geographically by asking yes/no questions (e.g., Are you in the Southern Hemisphere?). This type of experience gets all your students engaged and geographically proficient!

Reasons to do Mystery Skypes:

- Cultivates a global community
- Develops critical thinking skills
- Develops geography skills
- Cultivates listening and speaking skills
- Promotes student-led instruction
- Develops information literacy
- Provides an authentic purpose for research
- Promotes collaboration and communication
- Supplies challenge-based learning opportunities
- Creates global partners
- Develops netiquette skills

https://education.microsoft.com/skype-in-the-classroom/mystery-skype

PREDICTION #8: LEARNING WILL BE FOCUSED ON PROCESSING MULTIMEDIA INFORMATION

Developmental molecular biologist John Medina's (2008) research says that people can remember the content of more than 2,500 pictures with at least 90 percent accuracy seventy-two hours after exposure to the images, even though they only see each picture for about ten seconds. Recall rates of those same 2,500 pictures one year later are still an impressive 63 percent of the content of those pictures; however, the same research says that when people receive new information verbally with no image or video present—for example, if you made a presentation without including any visual elements and just talked at your audience—seventy-two hours later, members of the audience are able to recall only about 10 percent of that information.

Medina (2008) says this is clear evidence that the traditional stand-and-deliver lecture method is not effective. However—and this is very significant—Medina's (2008) research also shows that the percentage of information retained increases from 10 percent to 65 percent if the presenter adds an image to the new content after the fact.

Let us explain what is happening here. Since childhood, television, online videos, images, and computer games bombard digital generations with colorful, high-quality, highly expressive, realistic, multisensory experiences—sight, sound, touch, and soon even smell, taste, and 3-D—but with little or no accompanying text.

Images and video are powerful enough on their own to communicate the message to and for them. For people of all generations, but particularly for the younger generations (students born after 2005), the role of words increasingly is to complement the content of images and videos (Morrison, 2015). The result of this pervasive and chronic digital bombardment is to considerably sharpen the digital generations' visual abilities. This heightened level of visual awareness means that they are completely comfortable interpreting and conveying information in visual formats. Just try playing a competitive video game against a member of the always-on generations and you will quickly understand that his or her visuospatial skills are highly developed. Medina's (2008) research indicates that they have cultivated an almost complete physical interface between the digital and virtual worlds.

Meanwhile, 20th century learners struggle to understand this because that is not the world in which many of us grew up. We struggle because most of these older generations experienced paper-based training growing up. We learned from books. Schools trained us to communicate primarily with paper, words, and text. Our learning was primarily linear, logical, left to right, top to bottom, beginning to end.

So, what implications does this hold for education and educators? The world outside of school has already embraced visual communication. Allowing learners to work with video and other visual media to convey their learning allows them to create remarkable materials using video production tools that used to cost tens of thousands of dollars to buy but which are now free or inexpensive. As a result, their world has far fewer words and a greater number of images; and their brains have been wired for the fast delivery of content, data, and images from digital devices, video games, and the internet.

Current research categorically demonstrates that unless you're in the top 10 percent of readers and writers, you learn far more quickly and efficiently—and you retain far more information—watching video and then talking about what you've learned as opposed to writing an essay (Treadwell, 2016).

The same studies show that games outperform textbooks in helping learners learn fact-based subjects such as geography, history, physics, and anatomy, while at the same time games also improve visual coordination, cognitive speed, and manual dexterity (Treadwell, 2016). That is why some schools are now opting not to teach handwriting and are letting learners use digital devices to record their progress.

Imagining a world without heavy dependence on text is scary for those raised on 20th century learning. You might not like what we are going to say next, but you need to hear this: You need to understand that among the digital generations, visual communication is increasingly challenging the supremacy of traditional reading and writing. While reading and writing will always be important (at least for the foreseeable future), in an increasingly visual world, we believe visual communication and design must be an everyday part of the curriculum for learners at every grade level and in every subject area.

Modern digital media have fundamentally changed the essential skills we all need to be media prosumers (capable of consuming and producing media). Learners and teachers alike must be able to communicate as effectively in multimedia formats as 20th century learners can communicate with text and speech.

Make no mistake that the three Rs are still critical. However, traditional literacy is no longer enough. Both learners and teachers alike need to understand modern information–communication skills such as the principles of graphic design, how typography shapes thinking, the effective use of color, the principles of photo composition, the principles of sound production techniques, and the fundamentals of video production, not to mention how we use all these skills together to effectively communicate to different audiences.

#8 Processing Multimedia Resources

1. **YouTube.** Because YouTube contains a massive amount of engaging, video-based media in a single location, learners can search for specific topics and find a vast selection of relevant video clips. When users exercise effective research strategies, TeacherTube, Vimeo, and other video-based learning platforms provide instant access to more than enough video-based information to capture student interest in a topic. Learners, in turn, can become experts or teach themselves a new skill. If they are so inclined, they can upload their own videos, embed them on multiple platforms, and create their own channels with playlists for their subscribers to watch. Educators can use YouTube clips for instructional warm-ups, for new content delivery, or as resources for review. Another site, TeacherTube, is geared toward educators sharing their own videos and instructional resources with other teachers.

2. **Playposit.** Playposit allows educators to change how learners view and interpret video content. Educators find a video on YouTube, TeacherTube, Vimeo, Google Drive, or any of a dozen other video-hosting services and use Playposit to create student questions, conduct polls and surveys, or quiz learners about video content.

3. **Edpuzzle**. Edpuzzle is a video platform for both educators and students. It empowers educators to make any video into a lesson with easy-to-use tools. First, educators find, upload, or create a video (YouTube, Vimeo, TeacherTube, etc.). Next, educators stop the video at different points and insert questions, audio, text, and hyperlinks. After that, they share the lesson with their class and get students registered by using a "class code." After the activity, educators can review student participation and grade open-ended questions.

PREDICTION #9: LEARNING WILL BE COLLABORATIVE

Liz Wiseman (2014), a researcher, executive advisor, and writer, commented in her book *Rookie Smarts: Why Learning Beats Knowing in the New Game of Work* that "the critical skill of this century is not what you hold in your head, but your ability to tap into and access what other people know. The best leaders and fastest learners know how to harness collective intelligence" (p. 10).

Being able to collaborate with others on a project or task has always been an important skill, because by working together, a group can be more productive than an individual. The need for collaboration skills has increased considerably in the hyperconnected modern world.

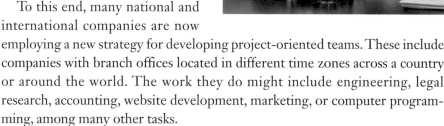

To this end, many national and international companies are now employing a new strategy for developing project-oriented teams. These include companies with branch offices located in different time zones across a country or around the world. The work they do might include engineering, legal research, accounting, website development, marketing, or computer programming, among many other tasks.

When a company has a new project, it is commonplace for it to create a work group consisting of people who live in the different time zones. When workers on the U.S. East Coast go home at the end of their working day, work continues on the project until the people living on the West Coast clock out. Work begins the next morning when the workers on the East Coast start their working day, several hours before the West Coast people return to the task. Taking this approach, organized teams can complete a project much more quickly.

Now consider what it is like to operate in this kind of work environment. In addition to having traditional team-working skills, working effectively within groups also requires a fundamentally different set of collaboration skills from those traditionally used when working face-to-face. Collaboration can now be either synchronous or asynchronous. Synchronous collaboration happens in real time. Virtual partners work and communicate simultaneously using a range of online digital tools. However, collaborating with virtual partners who are not physically in the same time zone often requires that some, if not all, of the work is done separately. This requires asynchronous collaboration, where partners work and communicate using collaborative software at different time intervals.

Collaboration skills include such traditional abilities as being able to organize functional teams with members who complement one another; being able to criticize ideas without criticizing individuals; taking responsibility for designated jobs; and negotiating within a team, which consists of group brainstorming, group problem solving, and eliciting and listening to feedback. Beyond these traditional skills, 21st century workers require a wide range of new technical skills together with a functional understanding of modern productivity tools such as Skype, Zoom, GoToMeeting, Google Hangouts, and Google Docs. Learning the skills needed to function effectively in virtual work groups has already become a new requirement for living and working in the modern world. The need for these skills will only increase in the future.

Consider the individuals in digital generations that are already working or about to enter today's workforce and how many different ways they have to communicate. They have extensive access to computers, laptops, tablets, smartphones, Wi-Fi, Instagram, Snapchat, Skype, Facebook, Twitter, texting, and much more. They know how to use these different tools for different types of communication with different groups. Because many of these tools have been available to them for their entire lives, the digital generations have completely internalized their use and take them for granted.

This ability is an asset that analog generations often misunderstand. In our experience, these generations often accuse digital generations of being digital zombies who lack even the most fundamental people skills. We disagree with this assessment. From our perspective, the majority of the digital generations are extremely social. They are just not social the way analog generations think of social. Outside of school, they are immersed in a participatory culture built on relationships that allow them to connect not only with their closest friends but also with people they have never met from the next town or on the other side of the world. The emergence of a collective intelligence on the web has created a global brain that has generated an entirely new way of processing massive amounts of data and converting these data into shared pools of knowledge, where the power of the collective whole is greater than the sum of its individual parts.

> From our perspective, the majority of the digital generations are extremely social. They are just not social the way analog generations think of social. Outside of school, they are immersed in a participatory culture built on relationships.

Schools must embrace the social outlets the new digital landscape provides. The emergence of a global digital network has shifted power and knowledge from the individual to the group. With the internet, everyone has become connected to everyone and everything else, which allows individuals to work together anytime and anywhere.

#9 Collaborative Learning Resources

1. **Padlet.** Padlet is an online, visual workspace that displays in real time the content users create. With a free-form or stream display, visitors add posts to a virtual wall. Anyone visiting the wall can see all the content users previously uploaded. Teachers, facilitators, and trainers are able to share a link and provide access to individuals and groups so they can brainstorm ideas, work on collaborative projects, curate hyperlinks to resources, take notes, create posters or brochures, plan events, and conduct online discussions. Padlet is great for all grade levels and content areas.

2. **G Suite.** G Suite is a versatile suite of online tools available through a free Google account. Having much of the same functionality as professional productivity suites, G Suite includes online communications tools, cloud storage platforms, and application types—such as word processors, spreadsheets, and slideshows—and provides a means for users to share access to documents with links and permissions, experience real-time collaboration and communication, and use collective intelligence to perform a shared task. Competing platforms from Microsoft, Apple, and others provide similar features.

3. **Online formative assessment.** Educators can easily fashion online quizzes and exit tickets using Google Forms or similar tools to dispense useful examples of formative assessment to learners. In a short period of time, a teacher can generate a survey to capture student performance or attitudinal data. Once learners have completed the form, their responses populate a spreadsheet that the teacher can view, download, and perform data analysis upon as the basis for future instructional decision making.

4. **Collaborative, real-time documents.** For a powerful, collaborative learning experience, provide small groups with a collaborative space and watch as text, images, and other content quickly populate the document. Teachers can easily scroll between documents to monitor the progress of different teams. Google also offers Slides, a slideshow generator that allows users to collaboratively build creative multimedia products.

PREDICTION #10: LEARNING WILL BE ASSISTED BY THINKING MACHINES, SMART AGENTS, AND BIG DATA

As learners progress through the grades, they will encounter a wide variety of teachers, some of whom will not be human. This idea of nonhuman teachers might make some of the over-forty crowd feel a bit uneasy, but for digital generations, who have never had a time in their lives where such technologies haven't existed, they take to this like ducks to water.

To understand what is about to happen in terms of the emergence of nonhuman teaching assistants, we need to apply our knowledge of exponential growth. We cannot make our decisions about the future based on what is in existence in 2018, because we know that the continuum of exponential development means that the emergence of new and more powerful digital tools is inevitable and always imminent. As we thoroughly examined in Chapter 5, we only have to look at what exists in 2018 and understand it as part of a continuum from the past to the future to project where digital technology might be when the learners now in kindergarten complete high school.

To consider the future of learning as it pertains to thinking machines and big data, we must

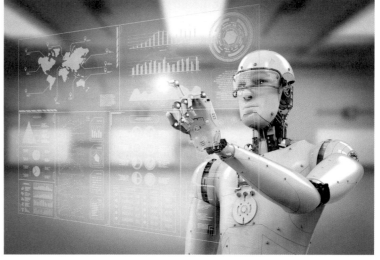

consider two key developments that will influence the direction that nonhuman instruction might take—expert systems and smart agents, and hyperinformation (information anyone can access anywhere).

Let's consider expert systems and smart agents first. An *expert system* or *smart agent* is a computer program that its designers program with general rules for its operation as well as the capacity to learn from experience (Brighterion, 2017). In this way, the program increases its capabilities to respond to specific problems based on situations it has experienced in the past and uses those experiences to make informed predictions. One example of this is an expert system programmed to diagnose engine problems in cars. These types of systems are connected to car dealerships worldwide via satellite. Each day, a person enters every problem a dealership encounters, as well as the way technicians resolved the problem, into the program. When a mechanic encounters a challenge, the expert system can give advice by applying the rules in its program, as well as by using its growing memory banks. In this way, the expert system becomes a valuable reference and learning tool that mechanics anywhere in the world can make use of each day.

This type of program could have an enormous impact on learning. For example, while doing research on volcanoes, a personal smart agent could take a student's verbal request, go out onto the network, and find all incidents of volcanic activity that match his or her criteria for time, duration, type, as well as any other attributes he or she might be looking for.

The smart agent would learn from experience how we ask questions and what information we were looking for when we phrased our queries in specific ways. In learning our personal habits and tendencies, the smart agent learns to make connections and inferences from the coexistence of two or more events with similar attributes. Imagine the power this kind of technology could have in the hands of learners of all ages.

These smart agents will do more than just retrieve information. They will also be able to analyze what they find. A student could set a smart agent to work at monitoring the stock market for any combination of simultaneous ups and downs in various industries, have it watch worldwide arms shipments and terrorist activities, or instruct it to examine the relationship between the destruction of the rain forest in South America and carbon saturation in the atmosphere.

The potential of this kind of technology to alter learning is not something educators can ignore. As we have stressed throughout this book, much of traditional education in schools involves teachers presenting learners with massive amounts of information they are expected to recall on demand. This leaves very little time for students to learn how to process, synthesize, evaluate, and apply what they receive. In an instructional environment that includes personal smart agents, this problem goes away, allowing educators to spend more time focused on the high-level thinking skills associated with evaluating the information students have their smart agents retrieve. Embracing this kind of technology represents an opportunity for a teaching profession that has long bemoaned lack of time and resources to teach high-level thinking skills and provide personalized learning.

Now, consider the use of smart agents in combination with the development of hyperinformation and smart devices. In conjunction with each other, these platforms have the potential to provide learners with access to personal learning systems that learn how they learn. Such systems can continuously adapt to a student's personal needs as he or she learns new material and encounters challenges. (Think of the iDEA Pad and EVA from the beginning of the chapter.) These types of technologies can greatly reduce the traditional lineup of learners at the teacher's desk.

Although such platforms are not commonly available yet, we are convinced the speed at which these systems will emerge will be breathtaking. Educators must immediately begin to prepare for new types of learning environments where nonhuman teaching assistants will take over many of the tasks currently done by human teachers.

We cannot stress enough that these kinds of learning systems are not a threat to skilled educators. Digital teaching assistants will free teachers from being the primary source of low-level learning to being the facilitators of exciting, modern-day learning experiences for students. These technologies can enable learners to independently learn the alphabet, the times table, spelling, and other such traditionally teacher-dependent tasks—all done with only minimal assistance from the teacher. Think of the freedom this provides educators to focus on high-level learning activities. The future will not see teachers replaced; rather, technology will create a needed shift in the teacher's instructional role from being the sage on the stage to being the guide on the side.

> These kinds of learning systems are not a threat to skilled educators. Digital teaching assistants will free teachers from being the primary source of low-level learning to being the facilitators of exciting, modern-day learning experiences for students.

#10 Smart Agent Learning Resources

1. **Social networking platforms.** Learning institutions are beginning to integrate smarter technologies into their programs. Similar to Facebook, Edmodo is a social networking service that allows learners to connect with one another to collaborate on learning tasks. It also provides teachers with useful tools to measure student progress and personalize the learning experience.

Unlike Facebook, Edmodo is *exclusively* geared toward education and is generally safer than at-large, public social networking services. Teachers take on the roles of facilitators and host their learners online to foster productive collaborative online learning communities.

Educators can conduct and moderate online discussions with their learners; construct and

(Continued)

(Continued)

dispense polls to receive student feedback; and distribute documents, access hyperlinks, watch videos, view images, and access other resources for student use. It also allows educators to recognize good behavior with an incentive-based digital badge system.

Using Edmodo, teachers have numerous ways to easily measure student performance and participation. Teachers can easily create, disseminate, and score assessment products such as quizzes and assignments using Edmodo's social networking platform. They can also use Edmodo's metrics for data analysis to monitor student successes and failures and react accordingly.

2. **Online editing apps.** Grammarly is an app and service for finding and correcting hundreds of complex writing errors—so you don't have to. As linguists and grammar lovers, we used Grammarly to perform initial edits on this manuscript, using it to scan our writing, receive real-time reports of performance, and view potential corrections while also receiving style instruction and access to tutorials. Grammarly also learns about a user's writing tendencies and tracks performance to help him or her improve.

3. **Digital personal assistants.** Digital devices and software have evolved to the point where voice recognition is exceptionally accurate and intuitive. With Apple's release of its digital personal assistant, Siri, more and more people are using new methods to search for information without typing on a keyboard. Similar products, such as Amazon's Alexa and Google's Assistant, have burst onto the scene in the past three years.

4. **Voice recognition apps.** Software such as Dragon Naturally Speaking for PCs and Dictate for Macs have been available for years. With each new release, this voice recognition software becomes more accurate and easier to use. With an incredible 99 percent accuracy, and a short, five-minute training session, humans and computers no longer need the tap-tap-tapping of a keyboard. Teachers can easily reduce the amount of time it takes to answer emails, type notes, give feedback to learners, or capture important information for those who are absent or are experiencing learning challenges.

For learners, speech-to-text allows them to multitask when completing routine cognitive work. Learners can record notes while they are reading and searching for relevant content during the research process. They can also give themselves spoken reminders like homework assignments, record ideas generated through brainstorming, or begin the rough draft of a blog post or creative writing assignment.

PREDICTION #11: LEARNING AND EVALUATION WILL BE HOLISTIC

How well do the assignments and tests we give measure student learning? Do they provide a complete picture of what a student can do? Or are we just measuring information recall and the ability to follow a set of steps in a procedure? Do learners understand what the information represents? Do they comprehend the concepts behind the steps they are following? Do they grasp the connections between the information they can recall? Does our instructional approach foster the development of deeper thinking skills?

These are incredibly important questions that every teacher should be asking about instruction and learning assessment. Unfortunately, educators frequently do not ask these questions, because they are consumed with demands they regard as more urgent. The overwhelming nature of the job, especially when teachers first start out, forces them to focus on daily tasks instead of pondering the effectiveness of their teaching and assessment.

As a result, many teachers adopt the *default approach* to instruction and assessment. The default approach is working within the teaching and assessment practices that teachers picked up when they were learners going through the school system. This approach is the long-established teaching-as-telling, learning-as-listening method of instruction that teachers follow up with testing-based assessment. This default approach to instruction and assessment is based on the following reasoning.

- A major goal of schooling is to help learners become productive individuals who can contribute to society politically, economically, and socially.

- A major aspect of being productive is to acquire knowledge and skills in several areas, including English language arts, social studies, mathematics, and science.

- A major focus of school instruction is on teaching this knowledge and skill to learners.

- A major focus of learning assessment is gauging how well learners acquire the knowledge and skills educators teach.

In this approach, the first step is to determine the body of knowledge and skill that learners should learn in a curriculum. Once the teacher sets the curriculum, he or she creates learning assessments to gauge how well students have learned the course content. Since the curriculum comes first, it is common in education circles to say the curriculum drives assessment. Most teachers are familiar with this model for assessment because TTWWADI.

However, even though this has become the widely accepted default approach to instruction and assessment, it has not always produced the kind of productive people that was the original goal. Instead, the focus on acquiring knowledge has led not only to teaching with an overemphasis on low-level information recall and rote memorization of specific procedures, but also to assessments that focus too much on test scores as an indicator of student performance.

There is, however, another approach to instruction and assessment that looks at learning from a very different perspective. This approach starts with the same goal as the traditional approach, but the reasoning then heads off in a different direction. That new direction is based on the idea that schooling should help learners prepare for what they will face in life after school. Grant Wiggins (1993) captures the thinking of this new approach to instruction by emphasizing the need for educators to provide engaging problems or questions of importance, in which learners must use their knowledge to deliver performances effectively and creatively. The tasks are similar to the problems and challenges faced by adults, consumers, or professionals in the field.

Here is the reasoning behind this new approach to teaching and assessment.

- A major goal of schooling is to help learners become productive people who can contribute to society politically, economically, and socially.

- A major aspect of being productive is to be able to perform tasks in the world outside school.

- A major focus of school instruction is on teaching learners how to do the kinds of tasks they will have to perform in life after school.

- A major focus of learning assessment is on gauging how well learners can perform those real-world tasks or simulations of those tasks.

We regard this kind of teaching and assessment as being more authentic because the learning activities in school mirror the activities learners will encounter in the world outside the school system. This instructional approach also inverts the traditional sequence of steps educators take to plan instruction. Instead of starting with the curriculum, a teacher must start with determining the real-world tasks that learners must master in a particular course of study. Once he or she knows the tasks, he or she can create a curriculum to teach learners what they need to know to complete those tasks. Authors like Wiggins and McTighe (2005) refer to this process as planning backward. In an article for Edutopia, Wiggins (2002) writes,

> We call it backward design. Before you decide exactly what you're going to do with learners, if you achieve your objective, what does it look like? What's the evidence that they got it? What's the evidence that they can now do it, whatever the "it" is? So you have to think about how it's going to end up, what it's going to look like. And then that ripples back into your design, what activities will get you there. What teaching moves will get you there?

This new approach to teaching and learning assessment emphasizes the application of knowledge to do real work rather than the traditional emphasis on just acquiring knowledge. This more authentic assessment gives a more holistic picture of what a student is capable of than what traditional assignments or tests provide. That is because authentic assessment does not encourage learners to simply do rote memorization and passive test-taking. Instead, authentic assessment encourages learners to develop what Ian refers to as high-level convergent divergent metacognitive (CDM) thinking skills as they do real-world tasks. Learners develop their analytical, convergent thinking skills as they solve problems, both individually and in groups. They must develop their creative, divergent thinking skills as they generate ideas for innovative solutions. Finally, they must develop their reflective, metacognitive skills as they self-assess their work and the process they followed to produce it.

In an authentic teaching and assessment approach, educators design the kinds of learning activities that learners do to mirror the types of tasks that people do every day in the world outside school. Here is an incomplete list of the types of activities that learners do in an authentic teaching and assessment environment.

Activities and Assessments in Authentic Learning Environments

- Solve real-world problems
- Form fact-based opinions
- Make recommendations
- Participate in debates
- Work collaboratively with real and virtual partners
- Read and interpret literature

- Write stories
- Do science experiments
- Make presentations to people inside and outside of the school
- Conduct social science research
- Solve mathematics problems that have real-world applications

These activities represent an authentic approach to teaching. They use problems as the primary strategy for instruction, and these problems have real-world links that lead learners into the kinds of tasks people encounter when they leave the school system. This approach stresses knowledge application to complete tasks rather than a primary focus on information recall. For many, this is a very different approach from traditional instruction—one that requires a new way to assess student learning.

Regardless of the topic, an authentic approach begins with the teacher identifying the desired knowledge, skills acquisition, or application he or she seeks when helping students to achieve the outcome he or she desires. When he or she identifies the outcome, the teacher then determines the most appropriate authentic assessment technique to use to measure student attainment of those outcomes. From here, the teacher can work backward to develop the specific learning strategies that will be the most effective in getting learners to the outcomes he or she targets.

In this type of learning environment, it is critical that, from the outset, learners clearly understand the expectations teachers have for their work. The best tool we have discovered for communicating expectations to learners is a rubric. Rubrics are invaluable instruments for helping learners understand what they must do to perform well on real-world tasks. A rubric is a list of criteria for a particular learning attribute. The criteria levels range from emergent to exemplary, accompanied with descriptions that explain what student work looks like for each level of assessment. The rubric, which the teacher builds based on his or her expectations for students, is based upon his or her goals for the project and the standards he or she plans to use when evaluating student work:

What are our goals? And how does this project support those goals and how are we assessing in light of those goals? So, you would expect to see for any project a scoring guideline, a rubric, in which there are clear links to the project, to some criteria and standards that we value that relate to some overarching objective. (Wiggins, 2002)

There are many tutorials and online tools that will help any teacher learn about and create rubrics, including the following.

- Rubistar (http://rubistar.4teachers.org/index.php)

- iRubrics (www.rcampus.com/indexrubric.cfm)

- Quick Rubric (www.quickrubric.com/r#/create-a-rubric)

We have discovered that having learners participate in the development of the criteria for the assessment rubrics is a very effective strategy for fostering student ownership of learning. This is something teachers can most effectively do after learners gain experience using rubrics for assessing their work.

As an educator, you can measure whatever attributes of learning you think are important. One of the great aspects of authentic teaching and assessment methods is that you can include skills and personal qualities in your assessments that are missed in traditional approaches. It is important to remember the old adage about the need for measuring what you want to see: "What gets measured, gets done. And what doesn't get measured, doesn't get done." This quote has been attributed to Peter Drucker, Tom Peters, W. Edwards Deming, Lord Kelvin, and others (actual source unknown).

If you want learners to follow a problem-solving process, then you have to give marks for learners completing each step in the process. If you want learners to develop their intrapersonal skills, then you have to give marks for that.

It is important to note that using authentic assessment versus traditional assessment is not an either-or decision. Traditional assessment tools like quizzes and tests still have their place in ensuring that learners have committed valuable information to memory. Many educational writers today advocate moving away from teaching and assessment that focus primarily on memorization. They cite research that indicates that memorization is a short-term skill. However, *memorization* is not a dirty word. You cannot talk intelligently about a topic that you don't know anything about:

Our line of argument is that testing is a small part of assessment. It needs to be part of the picture. Many people who are anti-testing end up sounding anti-evaluation and anti-measurement. A good test has a role to play. The language that we like to use is, it's an audit. It's a snapshot. (Wiggins, 2002)

Therefore, traditional assessments are part of a holistic approach to evaluating student learning. However, we must ensure that we go further than just measuring knowledge acquisition. We must use the strategies we have described here to assess skill development on real-world tasks.

#11 Holistic Evaluation Resources

Try to incorporate different types of authentic assessment during instruction. Some of these assessment types include the following.

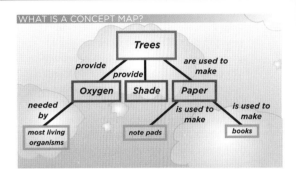
WHAT IS A CONCEPT MAP?

1. **Performance assessment**. In a performance assessment, we determine a student's ability to apply his or her skills to a real-world task. This is the kind of evaluation the world of work most often uses. "If you go into the workplace, they don't give you a multiple-choice test to see if you're doing your job. They have some performance assessment, as they say in business" (Wiggins, 2002). Performance assessments may require learners to work collaboratively and to apply skills and concepts to solve complex problems.

2. **Short analysis**. Short analysis uses a prompt to get learners to apply what they have learned to a short task. This can be an excellent way to assess how well learners have mastered basic concepts and skills. The prompt could be a poster, a political cartoon, a mathematics problem, a map, or a short excerpt from an article or book. Educators may ask learners to interpret, describe, calculate, explain, or predict. Visual representations of thinking can be very helpful in gaining insight into what learners understand. The teacher may ask learners to draw a diagram or picture that represents their understanding of a topic. Teachers can also use concept mapping. This is a visual representation of connections that can be a useful technique to assess how well learners understand relationships among concepts.

3. **Portfolios**. A portfolio is a collection of student work. It provides evidence of the learning a student has done over time. Thus, a portfolio provides a much longer-term picture of learning than teachers can obtain from snapshot assessments like single assignments, quizzes, and tests. A longer-term perspective effectively documents student improvement. For learners, creating a portfolio teaches them the importance of editing and revising their work. This, in turn, teaches them the value of self-assessment.

LiveBinders is a portfolio platform that allows learners to collect their learning artifacts into online binders. Learners can combine all their cloud documents, website links, and desktop documents to easily access, share, and update resources from anywhere. LiveBinders provides educators with the opportunity to see curated assignments to measure a learner's growth over time and provides a wonderful resource for formative assessment. LiveBinders is a tremendously versatile digital binder platform for online content curation and learning.

4. **Peer assessment**. Peer assessment is an excellent way for learners to get feedback about their efforts. It works best as a formative assessment strategy to provide learners with ideas for improving their product offered by fellow learners who are working on the same task. Because their peers are familiar with the challenges of the

(Continued)

(Continued)

particular task they are tackling from firsthand experience, their feedback can be very insightful and useful for learners in making positive adjustments to their work.

1. **Self-assessment.** Ask learners to self-evaluate the products they produced, the process they followed to produce those products, their participation in group activities, and their intrapersonal skill development. There are some strategies that students can use for self-assessment. For example, teachers can provide learners with a set of criteria and then ask them to self-mark their work. Give students some evaluative questions to answer, or ask them to maintain a journal to keep track of their self-assessment over time. As learners gain experience with self-assessment, ask them to become involved in the development of the criteria that will appear on the assessment.

2. **Cross-curricular learning.** Traditional learning involves learners exploring individual subjects—mathematics, social studies, science, and language arts. In the real world, problems and challenges are complex and cannot simply be solved by answering a mathematics question or a science problem. The real world isn't about disconnected silos of information. Mathematics and history and science and literature are parts of the same whole. This understanding leads us into the absolute value of cross-curricular learning (Greene, 2016b). Cross-curricular units combine subjects into a model that is experienced more in real life, allowing learners to see the relationship or connection between one subject and another.

Learning in the Future Digital Collection

Extend your knowledge of **learning in the future** by visiting http://bit.ly/BHCEF6. If you are interested in adding a resource to this collection of curated articles, contact us on Twitter (@ijukes or @RyanLSchaaf).

Chapter Summary

In this chapter, you read our eleven predictions for what education will look like in the year 2038 and the essential higher-order skills we must build in students today. As you reflect on this chapter, make sure you internalize the following key points.

- Some of the essential skills required for success in today's and tomorrow's world include problem solving, collaboration, communication (written and oral), research, creativity, data analysis, and applications of technology.

- Education must prepare learners for a global workforce that will pit them against equally skilled workers from other countries as well as apps, robots, and artificial intelligence.

- Schools must transform themselves from the traditional content distributors to cultivators of modern- and future-day skills.

- In the future, learning must be just-in-time. It must happen anytime, anyplace, in both virtual and physical spaces. It must be lifelong, personalized, learner-centered, and nonlinear. It must be whole-minded, real-world, and discovery-based. Learning will be collaborative; focused on processing multimedia information; and assisted by thinking machines, smart agents, and big data. Finally, learning and evaluation will be holistic.

- There are many strategies, apps, and resources educators can use or access to prepare learners for these educational forecasts.

Questions to Consider

- What will the future of education look like?

- How and what will the next generation learn?

- How will education prepare learners for a global workforce that pits their skills, knowledge, and expertise against equally skilled workers from other countries?

- As you look back on Alice's day, are there any ways you would alter the scenario to include a different disruptive force, technological innovation, or evolution in teacher pedagogy? Reflect on Alice's scenario and search for evidence of each of the Eleven Predictions of Learning in the Year 2038.

- Are there any other instructional approaches, digital tools, or instructional resources you would include under each of the Eleven Predictions of Learning in the Year 2038?

7

NEW SKILLS FOR MODERN TIMES

Our future growth relies on competitiveness and innovation, skills and productivity . . . and these in turn rely on the education of our people.

—Julia Gillard (2011)

AS we wrote in Chapter 6, education experts have developed any number of lists that attempt to identify the essential skills all modern learners require. Whether we're referring to Tony Wagner's (2010) "Seven Survival Skills," James Lengel's (2012) six principles of future learning in *Education 3.0: Seven Steps to Better Schools*, the World Economic Forum's (2015) "16 Skills for the 21st Century" in the *New Vision for Education* report, Ian's personal list (complete with more than fifty pages of categorized and sorted skills), or any of dozens of other collections, it's easy to be absolutely overwhelmed with both the quantity and quality of possible 21st century skills. So, how do we sort through the lists and reduce them to a manageable number? That's a question we answer in this chapter by figuring how we can have it all in achieving both short- and long-term goals, establishing our own eight essential skills of modern learning, and exploring the path forward.

HOW WE HAVE IT ALL

How do we address both the short-term goals of preparing learners for the national, state, district, or school tests, while at the same time addressing the long-term goals of preparing them for life in the 21st century? How do we address the need for students to learn the traditional content as well as simultaneously develop the essential skills of modern learning?

The first thing educators need to understand is that the traditional emphasis on literacy, while still very important, is no longer enough. We believe that even if we were to educate all learners to the established standards of 20th century literacies—reading, writing, arithmetic—our learners will only be literate by 20th century standards. They won't be literate based on the needs and demands of the 21st century. We believe that moving our thinking, teaching, and classrooms beyond the current focus on just 20th century literacies and helping develop in students the essential skills they need to live, work, and learn in the modern world requires developing in them a level of **unconscious awareness.**

As Noël Burch first theorized in the 1970s, there are four levels of awareness: (1) being unconsciously unaware (don't know that you don't know), (2) being consciously unaware (know that you don't know), (3) being consciously aware (know that you know), and (4) being unconsciously aware (don't know that you know) (Adams, 2016). The essential skills for living, working, and learning in the modern world are mental processes that we can help students learn, practice, develop, and apply so they can, in due course, become unconscious habits of mind. These new mental processes are essential skills that pave the way for success in the modern world. The major steps in developing modern learning skills involve conscious application of those skills leading to unconscious application of those skills.

> The essential skills for living, working, and learning in the modern world are mental processes that we can help students learn, practice, develop, and apply so they can, in due course, become unconscious habits of mind.

CONSCIOUS APPLICATION OF ESSENTIAL SKILLS

In a conscious application of skills, you can acquire skills, but you must think about how to use them. This is a very necessary and useful stage in skill development. Think back to when you were learning to drive. When you got your learner's license, you were very conscious of turning the steering wheel, stepping on the brakes, stepping on the gas, using the turn signals, checking the mirrors, as well as a whole bunch of other new driving skills.

Simultaneously learning these new skills was a necessary first step in driving. This is why we don't just give student drivers their licenses. They're not ready to operate a vehicle independently without an experienced driver being there to help them learn the necessary skills.

Since they're new drivers, they must constantly think about applying these skills, and, as a result, they don't operate the car smoothly. They lurch, stall, and stop abruptly. In the beginning, driving is a halting, uneven, uncomfortable experience. To become an independent driver, learners need sufficient practice and experience so they can learn to simultaneously apply all these skills in an unconscious and intuitive manner. Experienced drivers can perform these driving skills at a high level and still be able to carry on conversations with their passengers, listen to music, and sip on their coffee. They can do this because they don't have to think; they just drive. Learners demonstrate this when they learn a new mathematics skill or language mechanics or reading fluency. At first, they must consciously think about performing these skills. After practice and repetition, learners develop to the point where they can perform essential skills with little to no thought required.

UNCONSCIOUS APPLICATION OF ESSENTIAL SKILLS

Experienced drivers have reached a level of unconscious skill. When they reach this level, they're able to move to higher-level cognitive functions. They don't just respond; they also can anticipate what other drivers are going to do and take corrective or preventative actions before something actually happens. This unconscious skill level doesn't just apply to driving; it also applies to reading, writing, arithmetic, research, problem solving, or any other skill needed to develop practical intelligence. This is what conventional notions of multitasking are all about—being able to do several things unconsciously and simultaneously. In Chapter 4 (Digital Learners Prefer Parallel Processing and Multitasking), we referred to this ability as *continual partial attention*.

So, what are the essential skills of modern learning that students must acquire and develop on an unconscious level? Put another way, what are the critical skills all learners need to know to an unconscious level that are above and beyond an understanding of traditional content areas? We've asked this question hundreds of times in dozens of countries, to everyone from learners, parents, and teachers to educational and political leaders. In the next section, we detail the answers we found.

THE EIGHT ESSENTIAL SKILLS OF MODERN LEARNING

No matter who we talk to—no matter where we ask the question of what skills are essential for modern learning—the answers we consistently hear overlap with the views of such sources as Wagner (2010), Lengel (2012), the World

Economic Forum (2016a), the Asia Society in Partnership with CCSSO (Mansilla & Jackson, 2011), and UNESCO (Anderson, 2010). Education experts consistently identify the following eight essential skills they believe must become an increasing focus of teaching and learning if we hope to keep schools relevant in the modern, changing world.

1. Intrapersonal skills

2. Interpersonal skills

3. Problem-solving skills

4. Collaboration skills

5. Information analysis skills

6. Information communication skills

7. Creativity skills

8. Global citizenship skills

We posit that these are core attributes in developing what Carol Dweck (2016) refers to as *growth mindset*; that is, a mindset in which people believe their skills and abilities are not innate but something they can develop over time. As part of a growth mindset, students can develop these skills in the same way that they learn mathematics and language skills—with practice. They are the absolute foundation of everyday life and are embedded into almost everything we do.

The problem is that it is a challenge to introduce these skills to learners in an organized manner. For many teachers, teaching information analysis or global citizenship skills can become just one more thing he or she has to add to an already crowded curriculum. We find the best way to approach this is not to think of teaching these skills as separate from your curriculum. Our experience has been that the most effective way to introduce intrapersonal skills, problem-solving skills, and the others is not to introduce them in isolation; rather, embed them into the curriculum content so students learn them simultaneously with that content.

We believe these skills are as important as reading and writing were for success in the 20th century—as such, these are not optional skills. We call them the *Eight Essential Skills of Modern Learning*, and we detail each of them in the following sections (Jukes, 2017).

ESSENTIAL SKILL #1: INTRAPERSONAL SKILLS

Intrapersonal skills are internal skills, perceptions, and attitudes that occur within a person's mind. Art Costa and Bena Kallick (2008) call these the *habits of mind*, skills that individuals use to work through real-world situations. They are skills that allow individuals to respond using awareness, thought, and intentional strategy to gain positive outcomes.

Examples of intrapersonal skills include such things as self-esteem, open-mindedness, awareness of your thinking, the ability to learn, the ability to understand and manage your own emotions, self-confidence, self-discipline, self-motivation, the ability to overcome boredom, and patience. People who display these skills generally prove themselves capable of being a self-starter, being able to take initiative, working independently, being perseverant, having a positive attitude, and being a good manager of time, to name but a few.

ESSENTIAL SKILL #2: INTERPERSONAL SKILLS

One of the vital differences between intrapersonal and interpersonal communication is that intrapersonal skills are inward focused, whereas interpersonal skills are outward focused. Interpersonal abilities have to do with understanding and comprehending external situations and being able to communicate with others. Interpersonal skills are the life skills we use daily to interact with other people, both individually and in groups.

Interpersonal skills include such things as being able to engage in nonverbal communication, conduct a respectful conversation, give positive feedback, listen, persuade, debate, ask questions, convey social and cultural awareness, accept criticism, and demonstrate personal assertiveness. Having a well-developed repertoire of interpersonal skills allows individuals to handle challenging situations more effectively.

ESSENTIAL SKILL #3: PROBLEM-SOLVING SKILLS

Problem solving involves students learning a structured mental process that allows them to independently solve complex problems in real time. The world is in desperate need of analytical thinkers who can compare, contrast, evaluate, synthesize, and apply their analyses to answer difficult questions or

iStock.com/SolStock

solve problems in real time and to do this independently without instruction or supervision. The world needs people who can apply higher-order thinking skills. Problem solving requires learners to develop clear steps to solve a problem, unconscious habits of mind that allow them to explain; learn; practice; apply; internalize; and, most importantly, improve over time.

Ted McCain (2005) first developed this model, originally known as the four Ds, in the 1980s, and he later outlined them in his book *Teaching for Tomorrow*. Ian and his wife, Nicky Mohan, now expand the original four Ds to the following nine Ds.

The 9 Ds of Problem Solving

1. **Define:** Learners clearly define, restate, and communicate the problem or challenge. This gives educators the opportunity to provide formative feedback.

2. **Discover:** Learners discover the background and history of the problem, as well as the way the educator will assess the product and process.

3. **Determine:** Learners identify and specify the audience or stakeholders they will address or involve in the problem or challenge.

4. **Dream:** Learners dream, brainstorm, imagine, or visualize possible solutions for the problem or challenge. These solutions are not limited by time, ability, or money.

5. **Design:** Learners design a step-by-step plan that lays out the process they will use to create a product or solve a problem, thereby transforming their dream into reality.

6. **Deliver:** Learners develop and deliver a product and solution to a problem and present this to an audience of stakeholders.

7. **Diagnose:** Learners, peers, or teachers assess both the product and process and compare these to the original design.

8. **Debrief:** Learners revisit the first seven steps, reflect on their performance, and debrief the process.

9. **Decide:** Learners decide what the next steps are.

Describing the details of the nine Ds process is far too much to do in such a brief overview, but in general terms, the nine Ds parallel the structured mental process used in such things as the scientific method, the writing process, architectural planning, design and systems thinking, and how videographers plan and produce a movie. We passionately believe that problem solving is a process that educators must embed into every subject, at every grade level. This is the responsibility of every teacher at every single level from kindergarten through to senility.

ESSENTIAL SKILL #4: COLLABORATION SKILLS

We define it as a working practice whereby individuals work together to accomplish a common purpose. Whereas interpersonal skills relate to communication practices between individuals, collaboration skills relate to collaborative problem-solving skills when working in groups.

Collaboration is based on the idea that the power of *we* is greater than the power of *me*. In a fast-paced, high-pressure, online world, individuals and businesses must use every competitive advantage available to them. Even competitors collaborate with each other when it is mutually beneficial.

Collaboration skills include such skills as

- aptitude in planning and facilitation
- being able to organize functional teams with members who complement one another
- the ability to take on a role within a group
- being able to criticize ideas without criticizing individuals
- negotiating within a team
- group brainstorming
- group problem solving
- eliciting and listening to feedback
- taking responsibility for designated tasks

As we wrote in Chapter 6, modern online tools have greatly expanded the scope of collaboration to include synchronous or asynchronous communication. Take advantage of these tools to help students learn how to collaborate anytime, anywhere, with anyone (with internet access).

ESSENTIAL SKILL #5: INFORMATION ANALYSIS SKILLS

In a time of unreliable sources, we don't want learners who simply consume and regurgitate information without first questioning, analyzing, and validating the reliability of what they just read or saw. Rather, we want learners who can differentiate between reliable and unreliable information sources to determine

the credibility of a wide range of digital and nondigital materials.

We want learners to be information investigators who can consistently apply a structured mental process that is similar to the nine Ds we outlined for problem solving. Originally developed by Ian Jukes et al. (1999) in their book *NetSavvy*, we call this information analysis process the *five As*, and students can use the five As in the context of the following process to analyze and solve complex information problems.

The 5 As of Information Analysis

1. **Ask good questions:** In order to do this, learners identify key words, form questions around key words, brainstorm, think laterally, understand ethical issues, listen deeply, view wisely, speak critically, and distinguish valid information from white noise.

2. **Access data from the appropriate digital and nondigital information sources:** Learners determine where the information is; prioritize search strategies; skim, scan, and scour resources for pertinent data; filter information; take smart notes; determine when they have incomplete information; and know when it's necessary to go back to the initial *ask* stage to ask more questions.

3. **Analyze the data to authenticate their validity and transform data into knowledge:** Learners organize, triangulate, and summarize data; differentiate fact from opinion; assess currency; examine data for underlying meaning and bias;

identify incomplete information; document and credit sources; take notes; use probability; examine trends; and establish best guesses to seek out additional data.

4. **Apply the knowledge to solve real-time, real-world problems:** Learners synthesize information and turn it into knowledge with real-world application; such applications can include writing an essay, creating a graph, completing an argument, making a presentation, participating in a debate, completing a science experiment, creating a video, or participating in social media.

5. **Assess both the process and the product:** Learners reflect on the processes they undertake and information they obtain; assess learning—how they learned, what worked, what didn't work, and how they could enhance the process or product; and reflect on how they can apply the process to similar and different circumstances.

Once again, describing the full details of this process is far too much to do in such a brief overview as this. Suffice it to say that the five As represent a structured mental process that learners can use to explore almost any information problem.

ESSENTIAL SKILL #6: INFORMATION COMMUNICATION SKILLS

The world has moved beyond text. Visual communication through graphic design or presentations became the new standard many years ago—graphic communication is a given. Learners are growing up in a participatory and sharing culture—the YouTube era. In doing this, they have moved beyond still images to a new video benchmark. Constructing messages using an audiovisual standard not only requires an understanding of graphic design but also of video production tools. These tools, many of which are free, allow learners to move from being consumers to being prosumers—simultaneously consuming and producing media.

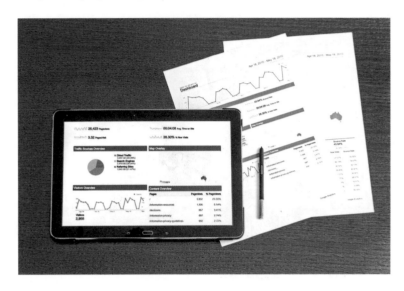

Because learners must be adept with visual communication, visual design concepts must be an every-day part of the curriculum at every grade level and in every subject. Learners must be able to communicate as effectively in multimedia formats as 20th century learners learned to communicate with text and speech. All learners and teachers need to know how modern readers read, the principles of graphical design and typography, the principles and psychology of color theory, the principles of photography, the principles of sound production, and the principles of video composition. They must know how to use this knowledge to effectively communicate information to others. Information communication skills are foundational and fundamental in the modern world.

ESSENTIAL SKILL #7: CREATIVE SKILLS

Creativity is about how you imaginatively communicate ideas. There is a rising creative class and a growing belief that creativity is an essential attribute that all learners need to develop. We can measure creativity, or the creative quotient (CQ), using the Torrance Tests of Creative Thinking (TTCT), developed by Ellis Paul Torrance (Kim, 2002). This test involves methods for measuring divergent thinking and other problem-solving skills and then scores the results on four scales:

1. Fluency: The total number of interpretable, meaningful, and relevant ideas generated in response to the stimulus

2. Flexibility: The number of different categories of relevant responses

3. Originality: The statistical rarity of the responses

4. Elaboration: The amount of detail in the responses

As has been seen with IQ tests, the Torrance Tests have historically risen around the world, going up about 3.2 points every ten years (Bronson & Merryman, 2010). This trend has not remained stable.

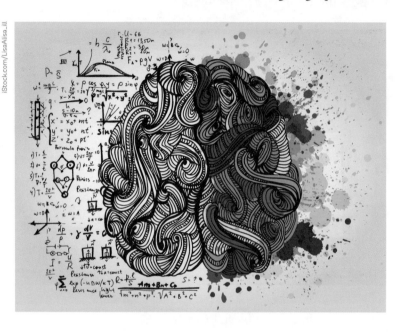

Kyung Hee Kim, a former associate professor of educational psychology at the College of William & Mary in Williamsburg, Virginia, analyzed 300,000 Torrance scores of children and adults taken since the tests were first developed in 1966 ("The decline of creativity," 2010). Kim's findings show that creativity scores, like IQ scores, rose steadily until 1990. Since then, she identifies a reverse trend, with creativity scores moving downward since 1990. The decrease is significant, but more unsettling is the fact that it appears to be accelerating, making it even more significant for scores of younger students in America—those from kindergarten through sixth grade ("The decline of creativity," 2010).

There is one crucial difference between IQ and CQ scores. IQ tests measure factors related to certain types of intelligence. The TTCT measures many different aspects of creativity, such as originality, abstractness, and open-mindedness. As Kim notes, "The TTCT measures the creative mind more broadly; it measures creative potential in many diverse areas such as art, literature, science, mathematics, architecture, engineering, business, leadership, and interpersonal relationships" ("The decline of creativity," 2010).

From 1984 to 1990, elaboration scores on the TTCT (scores showing the ability to create and develop ideas, to engage in analytical thinking, and be motivated to be creative) decreased by 19.41 percent. By 1998, they had declined by 24.62 percent, and by 2008, the scores had plummeted 36.80 percent from the 1984 levels.

It's too early to determine conclusively why creativity scores are declining. Kim posits that possible culprits include "the excessive time our children tend to spend in front of televisions and computers, watching programs, and playing video games, rather than engaging in creative activities such as playing outside or exploring the outside world" ("The decline of creativity," 2010). We theorize that another related cause is the lack of focus on creativity in our schools.

With the education community's continued focus on standards and high-stakes testing, many educators feel compelled to script learning to the point where they feel the need to treat spontaneity and creativity as counterproductive and disruptive. In some quarters, abstraction, open-mindedness, and originality appear to steal time away from preparation for the high-stakes testing that dominates our current educational environment. Under such circumstances, there may be little effort made to nurture creativity, primarily because it is more difficult to measure creativity than it is to determine learning as measured by standardized tests.

While this is happening, many countries are seizing the opportunity to invest in a culture of creativity by emphasizing topics rather than subjects. Most notable among these countries is Finland, which has long been highly respected and imitated for the quality of its education and the fact that Finnish students consistently score highly on international exams. Finland is rethinking how it teaches in the digital age, seeking to place skills, as much as subjects, at the heart of what it does (Garner, 2015).

We believe that Finland recognizes what many other nations continue to deny. All around us, matters of national and international importance are crying out for creative global solutions—from climate change, to the bleaching of coral reefs, to overpopulation, to combating terrorism and militancy, to the effects of droughts and wildfires, to delivering affordable health care, to shutting down out-of-control nuclear power plants, to identifying unreliable information sources. These endeavors require outside-the-box, divergent thinking.

We believe the currency of the 21st century is creativity and that countries that cultivate creativity are not only poised to offer solutions to these and other global issues but will reap the benefits of doing so. Countries that are creative are positioned to prosper, while the new third world will be the nations that have to import creativity like a commodity. Let us be clear: this isn't about some distant, murky future. We perceive that the growing demand for innovative and creative solutions is already happening. As employers continue to outsource routine cognitive work and manufacturing jobs, the only jobs left are likely to be creative-class jobs—the jobs that require high-level thinking.

In his book *A Whole New Mind*, Daniel H. Pink (2006) says that the wealth of nations and the well-being of individuals now depend on having artists in the room when anything is created. Imagine that—having artists involved in creative ventures. This sounds like common sense, doesn't it?

Pink (2006) tells the story of a professor who went to a kindergarten class one day and asked learners to raise their hands if they could dance. Their hands all shot into the air. He asked how many could sing, and again, they all raised their hands. Then he went into a college class and asked the same questions of learners there; no one raised their hand. His conclusion was that education is the process of teaching us what we *can't do*, not what we can do. We are all creative. It's not our creativity that's in question; it's our technical proficiency.

Pink's (2006) observations are further amplified in the book *Breakpoint and Beyond: Mastering the Future—Today* by George Land and Beth Jarman (2000). According to Lisa Rivero (2012), in 1968, the researchers completed a research study that tested the creativity of 1,600 children who ranged in age from three to five years old. This research study was the same creativity test Land developed for NASA to help identify innovative engineers and scientists.

The assessment was so compelling that he decided to use it with children (Rivero, 2012). He retested the same children at age ten and again at age fifteen. The results were astounding. They showed that the percentage of genius-level divergent thinking by age five was 98 percent. By ages eight to ten, it had declined to 32 percent. By ages thirteen to fifteen, it had further declined to 10 percent. At ages over twenty-five, it was just 2 percent. What Land and Jarman (2000) conclude was that noncreative behavior is learned, not inherited!

Why does this happen? During the process of development, we believe that children unconsciously start comparing their work and themselves to others. A little voice inside some children tells them they aren't good enough, and they convince themselves they aren't talented or creative. But again, we are *all* creative.

People often confuse the concepts of creativity and technical proficiency. As a result, they come to believe that they are not creative. We've all heard people saying that they don't have a creative bone in their body, when what they should be suggesting is that they lack the technical aspects of delivering their ideas. Be assured that you can create and you are creative; so are your students. We all are! Technical proficiency comes with practice. Just as we can learn technical skills, so can we learn the creative process.

> Be assured that you can create and you are creative; so are your students. We all are!

Although this is not a comprehensive list, what follows are some of the creative skills we increasingly identify as being essential for modern learners. These skills include understanding the problem to be solved, identifying key words and forming questions around them, brainstorming, thinking laterally, understanding ethical issues, listening deeply and viewing wisely, sharing personal knowledge and experiences, being able to move beyond what is known, using familiar and unfamiliar sources to motivate and inspire, seeing new possibilities, playing with ideas, experimenting, taking risks, and imagining.

Creativity is the most powerful competitive advantage any individual can have (Pink, 2006), and as educators, we must help students tap into that built-in creativity.

ESSENTIAL SKILL #8: GLOBAL CITIZENSHIP SKILLS

In addition to conventional, physical-world citizenship skills, society is placing an increasing awareness of, and emphasis on, what it commonly refers to as *digital citizenship*. As educators who teach learners in both face-to-face and

online settings, we believe we cannot focus on one without also focusing on the other. Instead of digital citizenship, we refer to these as *global citizenship skills*. We believe it is an absolute imperative to develop highly ethical, moral citizens who conduct themselves appropriately in both real-world and digital settings. Historically, introducing the fundamental tenets of citizenship has been an integral part of the K–12 curriculum. However, as the world changes, we must account for the skills necessary for life in a digital landscape while not devaluing the importance of traditional citizenship.

You wouldn't give the keys to your car to a sixteen-year-old without first showing him or her how to drive, having him or her obtain a driver's license, outlining your expectations, and identifying the consequences of inappropriate actions. Yet, in the digital age, parents and educators alike give children access to powerful tools and resources such as the internet, smartphones, and other digital devices without proper guidance—inevitably some of them make poor choices. It is incumbent upon us to provide learners with the guidance necessary to develop the skills they need to navigate the challenges of life in the modern world.

Global citizenship is about protecting yourself, protecting others, and protecting the work of others in both the real and online worlds. Global citizenship is a set of ever-changing social conventions about how people should act. Schools already do a pretty good job of modeling traditional citizenship skills. However, thanks to the digital age, we must also assist our learners in developing netiquette, demonstrating basic courtesies, and reflecting on privacy considerations. Each of these factors into establishing a commonly held set of rules and practices for face-to-face and online conversations, emailing, text messaging, web browsing, and social networking. More than anything else, as learners grow, they must cultivate a deep understanding of ethics and a sense of accountability that begins with the individual and expands to the global level.

THE PATH FORWARD

Although this chapter provides a thorough analysis of the essential skills of modern learning, there is still so much more to describe, like how we can embed and teach these skills together with existing curriculum content. If learners are to develop the essential, modern-day skills they need to survive and thrive in an ever-changing world and economy, then educators must also develop new mindsets and skills to reflect the realities of modern times. This is what we examine in the next chapter.

Chapter Summary

In this chapter, you read about the essential, modern-day skills students must master to thrive in the 21st century. As you reflect on this chapter, make sure you internalize the following key points.

- We believe that we need to move our thinking, that we need to move our teaching, beyond our current focus on just 20th century literacies to equipping learners with the essentials of the modern literacies.

- The essentials of the modern literacies are mental processes that students can learn, practice, develop, and apply so that they can, in due course, become unconscious habits of mind. These new mental processes are essential skills that pave the way for success in the modern world. There are two major steps in developing modern learning skills: conscious and unconscious application.

- The eight essential skills of modern learning are as important as reading and writing were for success in the 20th century—these are not optional skills.

- The eight essential skills of modern learning are intrapersonal skills, interpersonal skills, problem-solving skills, collaboration skills, information analysis skills, information communication skills, creativity skills, and global citizenship skills.

- The teaching profession must adapt and transform during these ever-changing times. If our learners are to develop these essential, modern-day skills, then educators must also develop new mindsets and skills.

Questions to Consider

- Why are skills so important for learning in the modern world? Why is content, although still important, not as much of a priority as skills?

- In your estimation, which of the eight essential skills of modern learning is the most important skill for learners to cultivate? Is there one skill that will become more important in the future?

- To what extent is education now addressing the knowledge, skills, and attitudes that are necessary for 21st century learners? What do we need to do differently?

- Play out the trends that we describe in this chapter over the next ten years. How will they impact students, especially those who are ill-prepared for this new world because they don't have the necessary skills? What are the implications?

8

NEW ROLES FOR EDUCATORS

You can't teach today's kids with yesterday's lessons and expect they are prepared for tomorrow.

(tweeted by Justin Tarte, 2015)

THE previous two chapters included several forecasts about the relationship between learning and life in the modern world. First, we examined what learning must look like for future success for all our students in modern times. Then, we explored what skills we must teach to help our learners prepare themselves for an ever-changing, globalized world. That said, a crucial question remains—what will teaching look like in the future? In this chapter, we describe eleven critical roles educators must embrace.

11 New Roles Educators Must Embrace

1. Educators must be future-focused.

2. Educators must be lifelong learners.

3. Educators must be learning facilitators, not sages on the stage.

4. Educators must be expert generalists, not specialists.

5. Educators must embrace discovery learning.

6. Educators must enhance instruction with real-world meaning.

7. Educators must broaden the perspective of the curriculum.

8. Educators must be evaluators of the level of thought.

9. Educators must teach to the whole mind.

10. Educators must use technology as a learning tool.

11. Educators must be holistic evaluators.

ROLE #1: EDUCATORS MUST BE FUTURE-FOCUSED

We have an important question to ask: Should educators teach learners the content relevant to just the current moment in time, or should they focus their energies on helping their learners cultivate the essential skills they need to

survive in the future? At this point in the book, you may think it's the latter, but the answer is both. As educators, we can teach the content outlined in our curricula and academic standards while simultaneously helping students cultivate the essential skills of modern learners—the same skills we outlined in Chapter 7 (The Eight Essential Skills of Modern Learning).

We are not asking educators to abandon all the tried-and-true instructional practices and strategies that have served them well for years or even decades. What we are asking for is experimentation—trying something new with learners. If you are a traditional lecture-based practitioner, then try problem-based or product-based learning, or experiment with the flipped classroom model, or explore game-based learning or experiential learning to introduce a change in your practice. A number of excellent resources can be used as a starting point by future-focused educators.

Learning environments have a profound impact on students, and by introducing new approaches to learning, both learners and educators explore uncharted and perhaps incredibly rewarding waters.

The New Media Consortium publishes an annual series of reports called *The Horizon Report* (Becker, Freeman, Hall, Cummins, & Yuhnke, 2016). The report provides predictions about what emerging technologies and trends have the potential to revolutionize teaching, learning, and assessment in 2018 and in the future. Previous reports accurately predicted educational trends such as distance learning, cloud computing, flipped learning, and social networking as being serious movements that would transform learning. The most recent report indicated the emerging trends include robotics, 3-D printing, artificial intelligence, coding, makerspaces, virtual and augmented realities, and big data (Freeman, Becker, Cummins, Davis, & Giesinger, 2017).

It is extremely beneficial for educators to both beware *and* be aware of future trends.

Resources for Future-Focused Teachers

Edutopia (www.edutopia.org)

Singularity Hub (https://singularityhub.com)

TeachThought (www.teachthought.com)

Buck Institute (PBL) (www.bie.org)

Vanderbilt University's "Flipping the Classroom" (https://bit.ly/1H3Beb6)

ISTE Games and Simulations Network (https://bit.ly/2pUfl2z)

#1 Future-Focused Educators' Resources

Abundance: The Future Is Better Than You Think by Peter H. Diamandis and Steven Kotler (2012b); www.diamandis.com/abundance

The authors of this book combine extensive research and interviews with scientists, innovators, and industry professionals to provide an optimistic look at how exponential technologies, do-it-yourself innovators, techno-philanthropists, and the rising billion are conspiring to solve society's biggest problems. Diamandis and Kotler have their finger on the pulse of disruptive change and its effects, both directly and indirectly, on the future of education.

It's Complicated: The Social Lives of Networked Teens by danah boyd (2014); www.danah.org

In this exploration of how teenagers communicate via social networking services, danah boyd provides a detailed snapshot to help us understand the complicated lives of the always-on generations. This intimate summary helps educators better understand the thinking and learning of their students.

Professional Learning Network: Modern Learners

https://modernlearners.com

Publishers Will Richardson and Bruce Dixon examine emerging trends in education, provide new perspectives on these trends, and outline strategies that help educators become modern learners and leaders.

Singularity Hub (Blog and News Aggregator)

https://singularityhub.com

The Singularity Hub chronicles technological developments by examining the breakthroughs

(Continued)

(Continued)

and issues shaping our future as well as supporting a global community of passionate, action-oriented people who want to change the world for the better. It considers emerging trends from the context of how they affect the way we work, the way we play, and how we learn.

_____

Thank You for Being Late: An Optimist's Guide to Thriving in the Age of Accelerations by Thomas L. Friedman (2016b)

Friedman explores why nations and individuals must learn to be fast (innovative and quick to adapt), fair (prepared to help the casualties of change), and slow (adept at shutting out the noise and accessing their deepest values). In his blueprint for how to think about the modern world, Friedman specifically identifies lifelong learning as being a foundational skill required by all to survive and thrive in the modern world.

ROLE #2: EDUCATORS MUST BE LIFELONG LEARNERS

Our professional and personal lives are filled with instances where we must learn on the fly or suffer consequences. Educators are no different—they must constantly learn, unlearn, and relearn to improve their teaching craft. Education researchers report new findings and advancements in teaching

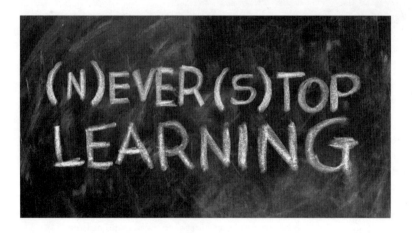

methodologies each day, but this new information, which is vital to educators, is easy to miss, awash in the sea of information overload. We must do better at investing in the future of our careers and, more important, our learners. Luckily, thanks to the digital landscape, an educator's quest for lifelong learning does not need to be a lonely venture.

As we have written throughout this book, there are thousands of collaborative tools that allow people to curate and share vast amounts of knowledge. The digital generations' use of Snapchat, Instagram, Twitter, YouTube, Reddit, and Tumblr to communicate, collaborate, and share ideas is creating an ever-expanding pool of knowledge. These tools all have applications for an educator's ability to engage in lifelong learning. Educators use Twitter and Pinterest to create professional learning networks (PLNs) to share ideas and resources, and educational communities such as Edutopia, TeachThought, and Edchat Interactive are just a few examples of teachers coming together to learn from one another.

> Educators must constantly learn, unlearn, and relearn to improve their teaching craft.

Challenges will never disappear, and they do not occur at convenient times such as during class, training, or a professional development session. Workers, parents, learners, educators—everybody—must be prepared to learn outside of traditional educational settings. Learning must never stop, and schools or colleges must not be the only venue for people to develop new skills and acquire new knowledge. Embracing lifelong learning is a personal and professional imperative.

#2 Lifelong Learners Resources

Mission to Learn

www.missiontolearn.com/lifelong-learner-free-resources

With an unprecedented abundance of useful learning resources and means for us to connect, communicate, and collaborate with one another, this site provides resources so that teachers and students can leverage learning in an intelligent, informed, and fulfilling way.

DIY Genius

www.diygenius.com/100-self-education-resources-for-lifelong-learners

The creators of DIY Genius designed their site for creative dreamers who want to design their own learning curriculum and create jobs to suit their passions. It provides resources for participants to experiment with creative projects and is an exceptional way for students to hone their talents.

"Learning and Earning: Lifelong Learning Is Becoming an Economic Imperative"

Economist ("Learning and Earning," 2017)

http://econ.st/2jbYV9N

Business affairs editor Andres Palmer writes about technology and the connections between education and employment.

"10 Reasons Why Lifelong Learning Is the Only Option" by Caroline Vander Ark and Mary Ryerse (2017)

http://bit.ly/2iBVwyR

Caroline Vander Ark at Getting Smart shares her insights into the ten reasons why lifelong learning is an imperative in a globalized world.

Authenticity = Lifelong Learners by John McCarthy (2015)

www.edutopia.org/blog/authenticity-equals-lifelong-learners-john-mccarthy

John McCarthy summarizes several educational practices for teachers to use to mirror the lifelong skills learners need to thrive in the modern world.

ROLE #3: EDUCATORS MUST BE LEARNING FACILITATORS, NOT SAGES ON THE STAGE

Despite the long-standing tradition of doing just this, our job as educators is not to stand up in front of learners and show them how smart we are. Rather, our job is to empower our learners to become independent thinkers. Our job is

to help them become men and women who are capable of thinking outside the lines and doing new and creative things—not simply repeating what other generations have previously done. The hardest-working person in the classroom should never be the teacher—it should always be the learners. For this to happen, educators need to shift the responsibility for learning to our learners.

If we continue to create a culture of dependency, twelfth graders will still look to their teachers to tell them what they need to do to pass the test, pass the class, and eventually graduate. After graduation, when we take away everything they have depended on, many of them fall flat on their faces. We bear responsibility for students who fail for these reasons, because from kindergarten on, we have created and maintained a culture of dependency.

> Our job is to help them become men and women who are capable of thinking outside the lines and doing new and creative things—not simply repeating what other generations have previously done.

Our job as educators is to facilitate in learners a culture of personal empowerment. Think about children learning to walk. When they first try, inevitably they lose their balance, fall, and land on their backsides. When that happens, do good parents walk over to them, point their finger at them, and say, "C–, you fail with a 27 percent. You've had five chances, and you don't get any more because you're not meeting the walking standards." Do parents write a rubric for walking without falling, or do they develop a curriculum to keep children upright? Of course not! Parents help them up, brush them off, wipe away their tears, and encourage them to try again. They do this because their goal is to help their children become independent—to help them to stand on their own—to make sure that they don't need us anymore.

Why is it that as parents we understand this, but as educators we don't? We must make an effort to progressively withdraw from learners. Our job is to make certain that by the time learners graduate from our schools, they don't need us anymore. We need to teach our learners to walk, walk beside them for a while, and then we need to walk away. In doing so, we cultivate a culture of self-reliance so they can make both a living and a life for themselves.

#3 Learning Facilitators Resources

What Is Flipped Learning? by Flipped Learning Network

https://flippedlearning.org/wp-content/uploads/2016/07/FLIP_handout_FNL_Web.pdf

This resource explains the concept of flipped learning and how you can implement group learning spaces to better facilitate individualized learning via dynamic, interactive learning environments.

"Rethinking the Lesson Plan" by Katie Martin (2017)

https://katielmartin.com/2017/05/26/rethinking-the-lesson-plan

As Director of Professional Learning at USD's Mobile Technology Learning Center, Katie Martin shares her insights into transforming traditional lesson planning to promote powerful, modern-day learning experiences.

"Try This, Not That: Make Over Your Lessons to Promote Student Understanding and Curiosity" by Nancy Van Erp and Diana Fenton (2016)

http://inservice.ascd.org/try-this-not-that-make-over-your-lessons-to-promote-student-understanding-and-curiosity

The authors provide some wonderful ideologies in line with modern-day learning to guide educators as they plan and provide instruction for today's digital generations.

"The Essential Underpinnings of Shifting to 'Modern Learning'" by Katrina Schwartz (2017)

ww2.kqed.org/mindshift/2017/04/26/the-essential-underpinnings-of-shifting-to-modern-learning

Using insights mined from Will Richardson and Bruce Dixon's call for a radical shift in education, MindShift's Katrina Schwartz shares an ingredient list for schools to consider as they transform to meet the needs of today's learners.

ROLE #4: EDUCATORS MUST BE EXPERT GENERALISTS, NOT SPECIALISTS

As we established throughout this book, academic success in the industrial age was largely based on a student's ability to memorize facts. Society highly regarded and rewarded people who could ingest and regurgitate large amounts of information. The challenge is that, in the modern world, memorization is just not the same as understanding. In Chapter 6 (Learning Will Be Real-World), we established that the current world doesn't need digital generations to be experts but rather expert generalists (HRreview, 2013).

This phrase implies that content specialization must give way to more general knowledge. In other words, as we shift from rote learning to more significant learning, we will witness a parallel shift from specialists to generalists who also have the effective information analysis skills necessary to deal with such transient information. (We write in detail on information analysis skills in Chapter 7.) This means that our success in the future will not rely just on what we can

remember; it will also rely on what we can perceive about the information we are working with, how we can turn this information into knowledge, and how we can apply this knowledge to address real-world problems.

Expert generalists study widely in many different fields, understand the deeper principles that connect those fields, and then apply the principles to their core specialty. *Fluid intelligence*, which is the ability to solve new problems, and *crystallized intelligence*, which roughly equates to an individual's stock of accumulated knowledge, have become equally important ("Old dogs, new tricks," 2017). This means that success is equated with applied learning rather than memorization.

For educators, this presents a significant challenge. Whereas in the old system, educators primarily focused on getting learners ready for tests, the emphasis going forward will be on helping learners apply what they have learned by solving problems and demonstrating transfer of learning to new situations. To gauge whether or not we are adequately preparing students, educators need to continually ask, "What are we currently measuring in our classrooms?" "What are we not measuring?" "Are there things that we do not measure that are essential to adequately help learners prepare for the world that awaits them after graduation?"

#4 Expert Generalist Resources

"Old Dogs, New Tricks: How Older Employees Perform in the Workplace"

Economist ("Old dogs, new tricks," 2017)

http://econ.st/2jLoVKc

This report examines how the human brain ages and observes that fluid intelligence and crystallized intelligence remain and even increase with age. In the context of education, it means all humans can learn, no matter what their age is.

———

"How Elon Musk Learns Faster and Better Than Everyone Else" by Michael Simmons (2017)

http://bit.ly/2zoH9bk

This analysis examines Elon Musk's personal learning philosophies and strategies as a successful expert generalist. One of the biggest takeaways is Musk's drive to continually learn, no matter how successful he may have been in the past.

———

"The Best Resources for Learning About the Concept of 'Transfer'—Help Me Find More" by Larry Ferlazzo (2013)

http://bit.ly/2hbH80a

Larry Ferlazzo collects and curates educational resources that explore the possibilities of knowledge transfer from one situation to another.

———

ROLE #5: EDUCATORS MUST EMBRACE DISCOVERY LEARNING

Have you ever watched a scary movie and had someone ruin the ending by telling you what was going to happen next? Has an online post or an innocent comment given away so much of a movie, a book, a game, or a story that you wished it had a "Spoilers" tag? In situations like this, we are often left feeling robbed of an experience, and the purpose of continuing may become pointless.

As we wrote in Chapter 6 (Learning Will Be Discovery-Based), learners experience something similar when educators overuse lecture as their primary instructional delivery method. Too much emphasis on lectures prevent learners from discovering new knowledge for themselves. In Chapter 6, we referred to this as the *teaching-as-telling, learning-as-listening* instructional model, which robs learners of that aha moment where they use prior knowledge and guidance from teachers or peers to discover something fresh on their own. We must constantly strive to be creators of engagement, not just content dispensers.

To be clear, there will always be a place for lecture and other forms of direct instruction. We are not suggesting that educators eliminate these instructional approaches. Cohen (2008) finds that both discovery-based learning and direct instruction approaches yielded roughly the same results. However, what is truly compelling about her findings (and those of others, such as Voltz, Sims, & Nelson, 2010) is the potential benefits of diversifying instructional practices to broaden learners' experiences and expectations. It is important to point out that the *teaching-as-telling, learning-as-listening* model only accesses the lower levels of Bloom's taxonomy (Anderson & Krathwohl, 2001). For learners to engage in higher-order thinking, they must ascend the taxonomy to the higher levels (see Figure 8.1). With discovery learning, learners are more likely to learn to analyze, critique, and create

FIGURE 8.1

Bloom's Taxonomy Verbs

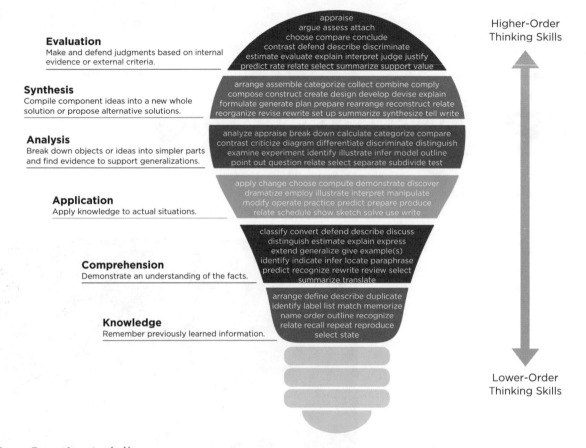

Evaluation
Make and defend judgments based on internal evidence or external criteria.

appraise argue assess attach choose compare conclude contrast defend describe discriminate estimate evaluate explain interpret judge justify predict rate relate select summarize support value

Synthesis
Compile component ideas into a new whole solution or propose alternative solutions.

arrange assemble categorize collect combine comply compose construct create design develop devise explain formulate generate plan prepare rearrange reconstruct relate reorganize revise rewrite set up summarize synthesize tell write

Analysis
Break down objects or ideas into simpler parts and find evidence to support generalizations.

analyze appraise break down calculate categorize compare contrast criticize diagram differentiate discriminate distinguish examine experiment identify illustrate infer model outline point out question relate select separate subdivide test

Application
Apply knowledge to actual situations.

apply change choose compute demonstrate discover dramatize employ illustrate interpret manipulate modify operate practice predict prepare produce relate schedule show sketch solve use write

Comprehension
Demonstrate an understanding of the facts.

classify convert defend describe discuss distinguish estimate explain express extend generalize give example(s) identify indicate infer locate paraphrase predict recognize rewrite review select summarize translate

Knowledge
Remember previously learned information.

arrange define describe duplicate identify label list match memorize name order outline recognize relate recall repeat reproduce select state

Higher-Order Thinking Skills

Lower-Order Thinking Skills

Source: Fractus Learning (n.d.).

new ideas. As the French novelist Marcel Proust (n.d.) writes, "We are not provided with wisdom, we must discover it for ourselves, after a journey through the wilderness which no one else can take for us, an effort which no one can spare us." It is imperative that we allow learners the opportunity to make their discoveries to bolster their curiosity, engage their interest, and promote their independence.

#5 Discovery Learning Resources

"The Effect of Direct Instruction Versus Discovery Learning on the Understanding of Science Lessons by Second Grade Learners" by Marisa T. Cohen (2008)

http://bit.ly/2Gy5mMB

Marisa Cohen finds there is no significant difference in knowledge transfer in a comparison between classes using direct instruction and those using discovery learning. Overall, results suggest that a mixture of instructional styles serves to effectively disseminate information and motivate students to learn.

———————

"5 Tips to Integrate Discovery Learning Activities Into Your Instructional Design" by Christoforos Pappas (2016)

http://bit.ly/2EJTHO8

Firsthand experience is a crucial component of the learning process. It gives learners the power to explore topics on their own and use their newfound skills in real-world situations. In this article, Christoforos Pappas shares some tips for employing a discovery learning approach to your instruction.

———————

"Hot Teaching Trend and Common Core: Discovery Learning vs. Direct Instruction" by Mercedes White (2012)

http://bit.ly/2EGCMIz

Mercedes White explores the benefits of both direct and discovery learning by citing both experts and data sources for support.

———————

"The Best Resources About Inductive Learning and Teaching" by Larry Ferlazzo (2015)

http://bit.ly/2FgMkLe

In the inductive process, learners seek patterns and use them to identify their broader meanings and significance. Larry Ferlazzo curates useful articles and resources for readers to introduce the inductive process and how to apply it in mainstream and English-language-learner classrooms.

———————

"Search vs. Discovery" by Robbert van der Pluijm, Rich Simmonds, and Mads Holmen (2015)

http://bit.ly/2OpCoFO

The authors explore the difference between search and discovery and provide advice for both learners and educators to embrace the importance of discovery in learning.

ROLE #6: EDUCATORS MUST ENHANCE INSTRUCTION WITH REAL-WORLD MEANING

In the age of InfoWhelm, we have exponentially growing quantities of data with an increasingly short shelf life. As a result, the truly gifted are not those who can memorize vast amounts of information as much as they are the people who can find the appropriate information and then apply that information to solve real-world challenges. Content will continue to come and go—only the mental processes will remain behind.

This is not to say that content is unimportant. However, it is critical that educators acknowledge and prioritize the need for learners to develop effective process skills in research, problem solving, communication (written and oral), and creativity. Educators must also be able to frame learning experiences within a manner that is natural for them to use content, skills, and processes

iStock.com/FatCamera

that best reflect how to apply content in a real-world context. To do this, educators must become process and context instructors, not just content dispensers.

One of the primary uses of information is in solving real-world problems and creating something new. For learners to undertake these endeavors, they will need educators to generate problems for them to solve or products for them to conceptualize and create. In essence, educators must be crafters of problems.

#6 Real-World Instruction Resources

"Solving Real-World Issues Through Problem-Based Learning"

Edutopia ("Solving Real-World Issues," 2016)

http://edut.to/2yDAE5l

The Two Rivers Public Charter School in Washington D.C., integrates problem-based learning at every grade level—pre–K through eighth grade. The school presents learners with real-world problems, has them undertake a series of investigations, and then helps them create products that they present to an authentic audience as part of the expeditionary learning education framework.

————————————

"Real-World Problem Solving: Project-Based Solutions"

Edutopia ("Real-World Problem Solving," 2015)

http://edut.to/1kN3lAQ

When designing projects and lessons at Crellin Elementary, teachers regularly look at school and community needs with the idea of using those needs as real-world catalysts for

learning, instead of inventing problems for the kids to solve.

————————————

"A Design Challenge to Learners: Solve a Real-World Problem!" by Ian Quillen (2013)

http://bit.ly/2G8yAm3

This site features creating a safe recreation space for teens, prototyping a recyclable lunch tray, setting up a water delivery system to guard against urban fires, building a public awareness campaign to combat hunger, and more. These are just a few examples of the types of tasks learners are taking on when they participate in the design learning challenge, an effort to get learners to figure out how to solve real-world problems in their communities.

————————————

"Top 12 Ways to Bring the Real World Into Your Classroom" by Kim Haynes (2015)

http://bit.ly/2dvt03D

Kim Haynes provides twelve suggestions for bringing the real world into the classroom for authentic learning experiences.

ROLE #7: EDUCATORS MUST BROADEN THE PERSPECTIVE OF THE CURRICULUM

As we have mentioned, the principles of mass production resulted in workers being assigned tasks to complete quickly and accurately, in a machinelike manner. Within such a system, workers were only responsible for their particular task. They were not expected to think or concern themselves with the bigger picture of what happened to the product before they received it, or after it left their hands. Similarly, schools divided knowledge into a series of separate subjects, conveying the message that that there was a single correct answer to every question; answers that students memorized rather than deriving on their own.

But life is a stew of interrelated experiences that students can better understand if we educators apply a holistic approach to knowledge, showing students the connections between what had previously been considered separate disciplines. It is increasingly important that we reveal the connections between mathematics, science, and language arts, and how the ideas in these separate subjects integrate with one another and the world outside of school.

Learners can sit in mathematics class and have a mathematics experience, but mathematics' role in life does not exist in isolation; rather, it's about how the mathematics of statistics, logic, probability, algebra, and trigonometry connect with music, science, art, social studies, language arts, and psychology. In true 21st century classrooms, it is likely that the mathematics department will become a sphere of influence that exerts its impact to varying degrees on the various tasks and problems that learners tackle in other subjects and vice versa. This is the approach that Finland took, where they intend for subjects to complement one another rather than for students to learn them in isolation (Garner, 2015).

Studying multiple subjects should happen without having to stop and think about where one subject ends and another begins. We must learn to teach deep, not just wide, integrating one subject with another and the world outside of school, emphasizing connections that are natural and meaningful. This requires us to embrace a much more holistic approach. (We write more on holistic approaches to assessment later in this chapter, in the section Educators Must Be Holistic Evaluators).

#7 Broadening the Curriculum Perspective Resources

"Integrated Learning: One Project, Several Disciplines"

Edutopia ("Integrated Learning," 2015)

http://edut.to/2zpiAe8

High Tech High School teachers find ways to collaborate and integrate content through projects that span different disciplines. Its teachers find that learner interest helps to drive their learning in many

(Continued)

(Continued)

academic areas, and when teachers collaborate and build a variety of connections into the curriculum, learning and engagement increase drastically.

_____

"Transdisciplinarity: Thinking Inside and Outside the Box" by Matt Levinson (2016)

http://edut.to/1OK5GVE

Due to the complexity of modern global issues, having one specialized discipline is not enough to tackle them (think water pollution or poverty). This post explains how multifaceted problems require transdisciplinary solutions, which are essential abilities for living, working, and learning in the modern world.

_____

"Why Every Class Should Be Cross-Curricular" by Kimberly Greene (2016b)

http://bit.ly/2haZbn7

Kimberly Greene shares her insights into developing cross-curricular experiences for her learners to infuse critical thinking skills.

_____

"Collaborative Planning: Integrating Curricula Across Subjects"

Edutopia ("Collaborative Planning," 2016)

http://edut.to/26eTojn

Hood River Middle School collaborates on projects across subjects to make learning relevant, connected, and engaging.

_____

"Deeper Learning: Why Cross-Curricular Teaching Is Essential" by Ben Johnson (2013)

http://edut.to/WmGkZs

In this post, Ben Johnson finds that educators have gone about as far as they can go with isolated instruction and learning. While it may have served its purpose for the older generations, he argues it does not meet students' deeper learning. Johnson outlines his process for engaging students in deeper learning with a clear action plan and resources to support educators and learners.

ROLE #8: EDUCATORS MUST BE EVALUATORS OF THE LEVEL OF THOUGHT

There is an old story about a tractor trailer that got stuck upon entering a tunnel. The truck was too high to get through. The driver, emergency responders, and road workers could not figure out how to dislodge the big rig from the tunnel's roof. Until a young boy suggested letting some air out of the tires so it could fit underneath the tunnel's opening. The suggestion is sheer genius in its simplicity. The young child was able to come up with a simple solution that escaped all the adults.

"If you assign a project and get back 30 of exactly the same thing, that's not a project, that's a recipe" (Lehmann, 2011). When learners come up with the same ideas or solutions to problems, they are performing convergent thinking. We see a lot of convergent thinking in schools, primarily because many instructional and assessment practices require learners to provide the single best, or most often correct, answer to a question. For example, $2 + 2 = 4$. "Convergent thinking emphasizes speed, accuracy, and logic and focuses on recognizing the familiar, reapplying techniques, and accumulating stored information" (Goodman, 2014).

In contrast, divergent thinking occurs when educators provide learners with problems or scenarios that are open-ended and offer many different possible answers. These types of instructional and assessment strategies encourage learners to think outside the box and demonstrate something unique. An example of this type of instructional task is to ask learners to create a public service announcement to inform their classmates about the dangers and implications of water pollution. Learners could research information about water pollution and select many different media to convey this message—a commercial, a podcast, a poster, or a pamphlet to name a few. No two solutions would look the same.

Neither form of thinking or teaching is entirely correct nor incorrect practice. Schools must focus on finding a balance between convergent and divergent thinking. Ideally, divergent and convergent thinking work in harmony with each other (Goodman, 2014). As educators, we must provide learners not only with opportunities to explore problems with a single answer (convergent) but also with challenges that require them to use their creative potential to demonstrate unique solutions (divergent). Divergent thinking is more likely to succeed in learning environments that allow for freedom in self, and peer expression encourages risk-taking, allows tinkering, and fosters learning through making mistakes.

#8 Evaluation of Thought Resources

"Fuel Creativity in the Classroom With Divergent Thinking" by Stacey Goodman (2014)

http://edut.to/1oqAyyM

Stacey Goodman offers his experiences with learners while having them apply divergent thinking (a way to generate ideas beyond prescribed expectations and rote thinking) to their learning.

"How to Build Your PLN" by Jacqui Murray (2015)

http://bit.ly/2hjrIKY

This resource, developed at Ask a Tech Teacher, defines a PLN and offers step-by-step instructions for creating one that will fulfill an educator's personalized, professional growth requirements.

(Continued)

(Continued)

Make Just One Change: Teach Students to Ask Their Own Questions by Dan Rothstein and Luz Santana (2011)

Dan Rothstein and Luz Santana not only make the case for the importance of teaching learners how to ask their own questions, but they also provide a clear, step-by-step process for teaching a sophisticated thinking skill to all learners.

ROLE #9: EDUCATORS MUST TEACH TO THE WHOLE MIND

To understand how to teach to the whole mind, we must explore the question, What does *whole mind* mean? This is an interesting and controversial question. The idea of the whole mind comes from the fact that the brain has two hemispheres with different functions in the thinking process. In the 20th century, many writers such as Daniel Pink (2006) claim that the *left brain* is responsible for logic and language, while the *right brain* is associated with context, synthesis, and creativity. However, as an understanding of brain function grows, it has become increasingly clear that these distinctions are not entirely accurate. Brain function in thinking is far more complex than previously understood. Research demonstrates that, in fact, both sides of the brain are involved in almost all types of thinking and that the left brain–right brain theory is a dramatic oversimplification (Medina, 2008).

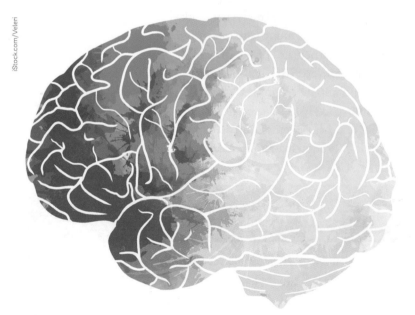

Founding president of the International Mind, Brain, and Education (MBE) Society Kurt Fischer (as cited in Bernard, 2010) states of left- and right-brain thinking,

This is total nonsense unless you've had half of your brain removed. . . . This myth was likely the result of a misinterpretation of the split-brain work of Nobel Prize winner Roger Sperry, who noticed differences in the brain when he studied people with surgically disconnected left and right brains.

Surely, some of us are more arts oriented or more science oriented, but this has little to do with some predetermined anatomical distribution of brainpower and more to do with environment and genetics.

A further extension of this widely held oversimplification is that the left hemisphere is associated with sequential thought and specializes in recognizing serial events like talking, reading, and writing. It decodes things that march in single file, handling logic and dealing with the literalness of meaning by breaking down images and events into their parts so it can analyze them (Medina, 2008).

In the same way, we perceive the right side of the brain to involve handling emotional expression and context, and putting the big picture together to create meaning. The right brain wants to take in all aspects of images and events simultaneously and weave them together to see things in context and create meaning because synthesis is what it does best. By synthesizing simultaneous items, the right brain resolves the contradiction, makes sense of situations, and determines significance (Medina, 2008).

In the metaphor "Joe has a heart the size of Texas," the left brain is associated with identifying the contradiction between the size of Joe's heart and the size of Texas. The right brain is associated with seeing the contradiction in context and determining the real meaning—that Joe is a very kind and loving man. The important thing to notice is that it took both sides of the brain to figure this out. Higher-level thinking always involves the right and left hemispheres.

For this book, we emphasize the sorts of whole-brain thinking activities educators must provide students as activities that utilize both sides of the brain simultaneously. Higher-order thinking skills and dispositions that thinking machines cannot easily imitate commonly describe whole-brain thinking. These include such skills as intrapersonal, interpersonal, problem solving, collaboration, information analysis, information presentation, creativity, and global citizenship skills (see Chapter 7, The Eight Essential Skills of Modern Learning).

Teaching to the whole mind also requires educators to recognize that learning is not as simple as a teacher telling and a learner listening. What decades of research and classroom observations show us is that each learner is unique. Some learners are strong in all aspects of mathematics and logic. Some are gifted in social interaction and collaboration. Some are great with their hands or can build, draw, sculpt, or design just about anything they put their hearts into. Some are excellent speakers and listeners. Some can remember anything they see. As educators, we must respect the fact that each learner has different strengths and weaknesses, and we must try to tailor our instructional approaches to simultaneously access their strengths while addressing their weaknesses.

Although a lot of the brain's abilities remain for us to discover, we have a far better understanding of how it functions and learns. We know that regular exercise, adequate sleep, and proper nutrition help promote healthy brain function (Medina, 2008). We also know that when we engage in activities that are complex and are successful in our efforts, the brain releases dopamine, a neurotransmitter associated with pleasure (Willis, 2007). We also understand that the activities that trigger the release of dopamine differ substantially between individuals, which affects how the brain processes information and how that information sticks to our long-term memory.

As educators, we must acknowledge that variety is the spice of life. It is imperative that we provide learners with a wide range of instructional approaches, strategies, resources, tools, and experiences to diversify and enrich their academic journey. Lecture, when used as one of a range of instructional strategies, is good, but educators should not overuse it. The brain loves patterns, sounds, and color—use them frequently. Incorporate instructional experiences that provide time for learners to work both separately and collaboratively. Try to add visuals to provide a better chance for the brain to store the information in long-term memory (Jukes et al., 2015). Change the academic setting by going outside, regularly rearrange the classroom, participate in field trips, and explore the real world through service learning and volunteerism in both digital and nondigital environments.

#9 Teaching to the Whole Mind Resources

Brain Rules: 12 Principles for Surviving and Thriving at Work, Home, and School by John Medina (2008)

In *Brain Rules,* molecular biologist John Medina shares how the brain sciences might change how we teach. Within each chapter, Medina outlines a brain rule and uses video to explore long-standing brain myths and explain what researchers and scholars know for sure about how the human brain works.

––––––––––––

"The Neuroscience of Joyful Education" by Judy Willis (2007)

http://bit.ly/1o12bin

Dr. Judy Willis, an educator and neurologist, examines how students' excitement for education wanes as they progress in their schooling due in part to standardized testing and rote learning practices encroaching on their innate joy for learning. She explains why many policymakers wrongly assume that learners who are laughing, interacting in groups, or being creative with art,

music, or dance are not performing work and how that leads teachers to feel pressured to preside over more sedate classrooms that produce lesser outcomes.

––––––––––––

Reinventing Learning for the Always-On Generation: Strategies and Apps That Work by Ian Jukes, Ryan L. Schaaf, and Nicky Mohan (2015)

This book examines how teachers and educational leaders can build modern learning environments to ensure student success in evolving digital landscapes. It explores the differences in learners' neurological processing from previous generations; examines the nine critical attributes of digital learners; and offers practical strategies for making learning relevant, engaging, and fun through digital activities.

––––––––––––

"Learn the Basics of Color Theory to Know What Looks Good" by Mihir Patkar (2014)

http://bit.ly/1paHnFX

This resource helps explain the basics of color theory and why colors are important to making things look rich and exciting, whether it's the clothes you wear or the presentation you deliver to an audience.

_____

Spark: The Revolutionary New Science of Exercise and the Brain by John J. Ratey (2013)

John Ratey presents evidence suggesting aerobic exercise physically remodels our brains for peak performance.

_____

"The Cognitive Age" by David Brooks (2008)

http://nyti.ms/2zquS5Z

Columnist David Brooks writes about why modern workers must become more effective at absorbing, processing, and combining information.

ROLE #10: EDUCATORS MUST USE TECHNOLOGY AS A LEARNING TOOL

There is a widespread misconception that technology is a subject or a curriculum, as if teaching Microsoft Word; PowerPoint; or various software, apps, or devices is an objective in and of itself. Often, people apply the term *technology* only to things that were invented after they were born. When writing, we don't ponder the pencil and wonder how it writes. We focus on the task. Likewise, we should treat current technologies in the same way. Technology is about using tools to help learners be more productive, whether those tools were created in the 1700s, 1900s, or yesterday. Think of technology as tools that help learners think and communicate more efficiently. If a digital device can do that more effectively, more precisely, or more quickly, then we should use it. It's only when we focus on the task that we can appreciate and understand the device's true power. If new digital

technologies can empower us, as educators, to do much more in classrooms than ever before, we must make a major shift in how we approach using them in the classroom. We must learn to let go of the mechanical things technology can do for us and concentrate instruction on the things that the technology cannot do. Instead of focusing on how to do a Google search, the focus should be on developing in all students the essential research skills they require to become effective, inquiry-based learners. When the focus is on the task, learning about the tool becomes nothing more than an incidental but essential by-product of the learning.

Some teachers find this sort of statement unnerving because they do not want learners to become too dependent on technology to do their spelling and basic arithmetic calculations. Although 20th century learners may be able to add, subtract, divide, and multiply better than a student will in the future, it is also true that future students will be able to do these operations faster and more accurately using digital technology. There is still an absolute need to understand the principles of mathematics, but there is also a very practical value in using the tools we have at hand.

We must stop teaching things such as keyboarding, word processing, or coding as entirely separate subjects. Rather, we should treat these skills as incidental and embed them in our teaching of the writing process, whether we're writing for language arts, science, or social studies. When we do so, we'll find that technology will slide into the incidental, unremarkable background of the classroom.

Educators must get over the fear that technology will replace them. We have said this already, but it bears repeating—any teacher who can be replaced by a computer deserves to be replaced. Any classroom device requires the vision and understanding of an inspired educator in order for anything of value to happen. Education is a human task that involves improving the human condition—only humans can do that.

#10 Technology as a Learning Tool Resources

"Ray Kurzweil's Wildest Prediction: Nanobots Will Plug Our Brains Into the Web by the 2030s" by Peter Diamandis (2015)

http://bit.ly/2lYPQ6W

Peter Diamandis shares many of Ray Kurzweil's predictions for a future filled with exciting advances in technology and human potential. Many of his predictions have strong implications for the future of learning such as knowledge transfer and downloadable experiences.

———————————

"Teaching 21st Century Skills Requires More Than Just Technology" by Beth Holland (2017)

http://bit.ly/2rjEX1h

Beth Holland makes the clear distinction between technology use and cultivating 21st century skills and why it's not enough for students to be able to use tools from sources like Google, Microsoft, Apple, and Amazon if they're not also netting the life skills necessary to learn and produce great content.

———————————

10 Principles for Schools of Modern Learning by Will Richardson and Bruce Dixon (2017)

http://bit.ly/2kmTO7i

This twenty-page ebook provides readers with a framework for developing students into deep, powerful, curious, and agile learners. It provides action steps to inform process changes in your school and links to resources you and your stakeholders can access to get started.

———————————

"Looking Ahead as Moore's Law Turns 50: What's Next for Computing?" by Jason Dorrier (2015)

http://bit.ly/2j6m67h

Jason Dorrier theorizes what could potentially be the next breakthrough in computing technology. Consider this information and how it reflects that learners will continue to have access to devices that are ever more powerful, faster, and cheaper.

ROLE #11: EDUCATORS MUST BE HOLISTIC EVALUATORS

Our educational system has traditionally placed a great deal of emphasis on standardized testing—testing that primarily focuses on one particular type of intelligence and one aspect of learning. Cornell University psychologist Robert J. Sternberg's (1985) triarchic theory of intelligence "identifies three kinds of smarts: the analytic type reflected in IQ scores; practical intelligence, which is more relevant for real-life problem solving; and creativity" (Wallis, 2017). Standardized tests are tools that measure only one specific type of intelligence—the analytical. Although analytical intelligence is very important, the mandate of schools must be to prepare learners for their futures, which requires them to develop the other two types of intelligence just as intensely—practical and creativity.

Practical intelligence involves what many refer to as *street smarts*. This intelligence involves a person adapting to the situation or environment; shaping the situation or environment to meet his or her needs or solve a problem; and selecting a new situation or environment to replace the old or less optimal one.

Creativity intelligence involves divergent thinking. This involves the ability of a person to generate new ideas or solutions to a problem he or she has never experienced before. The person also automates a process to the point that he or she is adept at it and can perform the same function with less and less cognitive effort.

The question is, do current standardized tests such as the Scholastic Aptitude Test (SAT), American College Test (ACT), Graduate Record Examination (GRE), tests of general educational development (GED), and Miller Analogies Test (MAT) measure practical or creativity intelligence? The education community may consider them excellent tools for measuring analytical intelligence, but they do very little to measure higher-order thinking and creativity. They represent only a single snapshot of a person's true ability and potential.

Our current assessments are geared toward reporting on mastery—often what the grade measures—rather than learning. But we could create assessments that value the learning along the way. Such a system would record not just quizzes, tests, written work, and presentations, but also exit tickets, and even conversations between student and teacher (Miller, 2017).

Holistic evaluation combines standardized testing with a wide variety of formal and informal means of evaluation. These include quantitative and qualitative, summative and formative, self and peer, performance-based and outcomes-based, and product- and process-based assessments.

Educators today must demand multiple snapshots that reflect the whole picture, the whole slideshow, the whole album, and the learner's whole movie. This means engaging in diverse forms of not just summative assessment but also ongoing and proactive informal and formal formative assessment. *Summative assessment* occurs at the end of the instructional process. *Formative assessment* is ongoing, and both teachers and learners use it to evaluate and make adjustments during the learning process. Formative assessment is a critical way for teachers to check learners' understanding and then use the information to guide future instruction. It helps create and renew the learning process.

Unlike the linear design of summative assessment, formative assessment is more like a cycle. Educators continuously guide learners to access their prior knowledge, engage them in learning activities to build on their knowledge base, help them to demonstrate their instructional gains (through a variety of assessment methods), and then reflect on the learning.

After completing this cycle, the entire process begins anew. Formative assessments come in all shapes and sizes: exit tickets or slips, learner portfolios, written evidence, journals, performance assessment tasks, games, learner observations, anecdotal notes, surveys, polls, role plays and skits, posters, infographics, sculptures, and paintings, to name a few.

To understand and truly evaluate modern-day learners, we must use these assessment forms to better see the whole picture, the whole person, the whole mind, and the whole learner. Without any of this, we are left with an incomplete puzzle.

#11 Holistic Evaluators Resources

"100 Things Students Can Create to Demonstrate What They Know" by Ryan L. Schaaf (2014b)

http://bit.ly/2AhWckm

Many educators use the same strategies over and over in their lessons, causing a rut in instruction. Variety is the spice of life! Learners benefit from being able to express themselves and their learning in a variety of different ways. They want their academic work to be relevant, engaging, and fun. This post includes one hundred ideas for educators to consider using with learners.

"Take Three! 55 Digital Tools and Apps for Formative Assessment Success" by Kathy Dyer (2016)

http://bit.ly/2zjWSJd

This post lists fifty-five digital tools and apps for formative assessment success.

_____

Beyond IQ: A Triarchic Theory of Intelligence by Robert J. Sternberg (1985)

This book presents a "triarchic" theory of human intelligence that goes beyond IQ in its conceptualization and implications for assessment. Sternberg's theory of intelligence provides educators with a firm reminder that intelligence goes far beyond what learners can memorize from a book or complete on a test.

_____

"34 Strategies for the Stages of Assessment: Before, During and After" (n.d.)

http://bit.ly/2hQ7Fk9

This post offers thirty-four strategies for each stage of the assessment process—before, during, and after. It also explains the purpose and function for each of these stages as they reflect the learning process.

_____

"How to Find the Middle Ground Between Data-Driven and Student-Driven Learning in Your Classroom" by Nira Dale (2016)

http://bit.ly/2yf7hli

Nira Dale discusses the balance between a data-driven and student-driven instructional program. She suggests empowering learners with more choice and using their interests to reach them.

New Roles of Educators Digital Collection

Extend your knowledge of **New Roles of Educators** by visiting http://bit.ly/BHCEF8. If you are interested in adding a resource to this collection of curated articles, contact us on Twitter (@ijukes or @RyanLSchaaf).

Chapter Summary

In this chapter, you read about the essential roles educators must play to remain effective teachers in the 21st century. As you reflect on this chapter, make sure you internalize the following eleven key roles.

1. Educators must be future-focused.

2. Educators must be lifelong learners.

3. Educators must be facilitators of learning, not sages on the stage.

4. Educators must be expert generalists, not specialists.

5. Educators must embrace discovery learning.

6. Educators must enhance instruction with real-world meaning.

7. Educators must broaden the perspective of the curriculum.

8. Educators must be evaluators of the level of thought.

9. Educators must teach to the whole mind.

10. Educators must use technology as a learning tool.

11. Educators must be holistic evaluators.

Questions to Consider

- What are some other critical roles you feel educators must embrace for the future of teaching that the education community at large has not identified?

- Are there books, online communities, tools, or other web resources that align with one or more of the roles we spotlighted in this chapter that we haven't identified? We invite you to share these resources with readers of the book (Twitter @ijukes or @RyanLSchaaf).

- Are any of the roles we identified in this chapter more critical than others? If so, why and what are they?

- As an educator, what roles do you feel you are most adept in? What roles must you further develop?

EPILOGUE

WHERE WE BEGIN

It is the business of the future to be dangerous. The major advances in civilization are processes that all but wreck the societies in which they occur.

—Alfred North Whitehead (1967)

One of the most significant challenges we face is that in disruptive times, society no longer measures the long term in centuries, decades, or even years—sometimes dramatic changes happen in a matter of months, weeks, days, or even hours. We live in a time wherein change is accelerating so much that we only really begin to see the present when it is already disappearing into the past.

As a result, our biggest challenge, both professionally and personally, is and will continue to be not just acknowledging but also accepting the scale of change we all face. We are experiencing change that is happening so rapidly that even the very nature and definition of change is changing. But when changes occur rapidly, as is the case here, we often tend to want to hang on to old ideas, TTWWADI mindsets, traditions, and worldviews.

In planning and writing this book, our greatest fear has and continues to be that, despite society's very best intentions to do what is right for its children and nations, educators and education stakeholders are unintentionally doing a terrific job of preparing students for a world that increasingly does not exist.

If we do not reinvent education, we, as nations, organizations, communities, and individuals, will not be prepared to face a future that will be complex, disruptive, and fraught with massive change and innovation. That is the real challenge that education and educators face. We acknowledge that change is hard, and we know that sometimes the challenge of change can seem utterly overwhelming. So, how do we deal with such fast-paced change? How do we deal with TTWWADI? How do we deal with terminal paradigm paralysis?

We both passionately believe that, as educators, this cannot be about us, our issues, needs, or comfort zones; rather, this is about our students and children and our hopes, dreams, and prayers for their futures. They may only be 20 percent of the population, but they are 1,000 percent of the future of every country. If we don't maximize students' opportunities to succeed, we fail as a society. We're fooling ourselves if we think we are going to sustain our economies with McJobs and McSkills. Futurist Bob Hughes's quote in Chapter 3 bears repeating, "In the culture of the 21st century, everything from the neck down will be minimum wage" (personal communication, 1996). Everything that can be automated, turned into hardware or software, outsourced, or offshored will pay minimum wage. So, we have a choice—either our citizens have high-level skills, or they get low wages. If they don't develop those skills in our schools, we have failed them.

We hear complaints all the time that kids today are different and that our schools aren't what they used to be. Frankly, we believe the problem with our schools is that they *are* what they used to be. Culturally, cognitively, and socially, the digital generations are different from their predecessors, but structurally, our schools are just like they were in the 20th century.

If we are going to help our learners prepare themselves for their futures and not just their parents' past, we are going to need new ways of educating within our schools. More than that, educators are going to need new mindsets. Economic, technological, informational, demographic, and political forces have and continue to transform the way people live and work. These changes and the rate of change will continue to accelerate. Our schools, just like our businesses, communities, and families, must continually adapt to changing conditions not to just survive, but to thrive. We need new schools for the new world. Schools that will prepare learners for life after school and the rest of their lives.

As educators, our challenge is not just to maintain what is or has been. Our job is also to shape what can be, what might be, what must be. We acknowledge that it is normal to be overwhelmed. The change process is messy and doesn't happen overnight.

THE COMMITTED SARDINE

Change is hard, and it is very easy to become overwhelmed by the challenges we face every day. Whenever Ian feels overwhelmed, he likes to visit the Monterey Bay Aquarium in Monterey, California—the world's greatest aquarium, in Ian's

humble opinion. During one such visit, the gift shop was showing a video about blue whales. Blue whales are the largest mammals on the planet. A blue whale weighs more than a fully loaded 737 airplane. It is the length of about three school buses put end-to-end. It has a heart the size of Volkswagen Beetle and a tongue that is eight feet long. A single adult blue whale consumes four tons of krill a day (whalefacts.org). Experts estimate that a baby blue whale gains fifteen pounds an hour during its first year of life. Another little-known fact about blue whales is that they are so mammoth that if one is swimming in one direction and wants to turn in another direction, it takes it three to five minutes to turn 180 degrees. A very strong parallel can be drawn between blue whales and our existing school systems. Both seem to take forever to turn around.

If you walk past the video on blue whales in the gift shop, turn to the left, and walk about fifty yards farther on, you come to what Ian considers to be the absolute centerpiece of the Monterey Bay Aquarium—a ten-story, all-glass tank, inside of which the aquarium staff placed many of the creatures that are indigenous to the Monterey Bay. If you've ever read *Cannery Row* (Steinbeck, 1945), you will know that in the first half of the 20th century, twice a year, in the inner Monterey Bay, there used to appear, out of nowhere, schools of fish—actually schools of sardines—that were the length, the width, and the depth of city blocks. Schools of sardines that had a mass not of one, two, or three blue whales but of a thousand (McCain & Jukes, 2000).

There is a fundamental difference between the way a blue whale turns around and the way a school of sardines turns around—which is instantly. How do the sardines do it? How do they know when to turn? Is it extrasensory perception? Is it Twitter? Are they using Facebook or Snapchat? Because Ian was curious, he pressed his nose against the glass of the tank and looked inside at the massive school of sardines that was swimming around inside. At first, the sardines appeared to be all swimming in the same direction. However, after a while, as his eyes adjusted to the light, he began to realize, slowly at first, that at any one time, there would be a small group of sardines swimming in another direction—and when they did, they caused conflict, discomfort, and distress.

When the school reached a critical mass of truly committed sardines—not 50 or 60 percent of the sardines who wanted to change but 10 to 15 percent who truly believed in change—the rest of the school instantly turned and followed. This is exactly what has happened since the 1960s with society's perspectives on things such as tobacco, the unacceptability of drinking and driving, the emergence of social media, or concern about climate change. Each one of these attitude shifts seemed to happen overnight, but in fact, they were all years in the making.

Our question is, Who among you is willing to become a *committed sardine*? Who among you is willing to swim against the flow, against conventional wisdom, against our long-standing and traditional TTWWADI-based practices and assumptions about education, and begin to move our schools, learners, and communities from where they are to where they need to be? Margaret Mead (1901–1978) is often quoted as saying, "Never doubt that a small group of thoughtful, committed citizens can change the world—indeed it is the only thing that ever has" (2005, p. 12). We heartily agree.

The bottom line is that change doesn't start with your president or prime minister. It doesn't start with your governor or premier. It doesn't start with your mayor or county executive. It doesn't start with your superintendent or your principal. Change starts with you. Change starts with us. Change starts here. Change starts now. We can't all change at once, and we can't just wait for everyone else to change first. The longest journey starts with a single step; the greatest movement starts with a single individual. If it is going to be, it is up to me, it is up to you, it's up to all of us together.

> Who among you is willing to become a *committed sardine*? Who among you is willing to swim against the flow, against conventional wisdom, against our long-standing and traditional TTWWADI-based practices and assumptions about education?

If we are going to uncover the full intellectual and creative genius of all our nations' learners, it is you—it is educators and educational leaders—who are going to make it happen. You have the hardest jobs in the world. That's because you are the facilitators of knowledge for millions of students who are growing up in the Knowledge Age. Modern education alone stands in the gap between their present and their future, between their failure and their fulfillment. So, you must believe us when we say that it is your energy—it is your passion—it is your creativity, commitment, and hard work every day that build a bridge so that our nations' students can cross the gap between the present and the future. As our students cross that gap, so do entire nations. You are the world's greatest hope—you are its most important professionals!

Next Steps for Education Digital Collection

To continue your **professional and personal growth** as an educator, we set up an Evernote notebook with a curated collection of articles to help you continue to take steps to answer the call and educate learners for their futures. Visit http://bit.ly/BHCEF9 to review these resources.

Questions to Consider

- How do we in education deal with such fast-paced change?

- How do we deal with the TTWWADI mentality in schools today?

- How do we deal with terminal paradigm paralysis?

- Why are a few brave educators and leaders such a powerful reckoning for change in our schools?

- Are you willing to become a *committed sardine*? Who can you convince to join you?

REFERENCES AND RESOURCES

Adams, L. (2016). Learning a new skill is easier said than done. *Gordon Training International*. Retrieved from http://www.gordontraining.com/free-workplace-articles/learning-a-new-skill-is-easier-said-than-done/

Amadeo, K. (2017, March 30). *How outsourcing jobs affects the U.S. economy*. Retrieved September 20, 2017, from www.thebalance.com/how-outsourcing-jobs-affects-the-u-s-economy-3306279

Amazon. (2016, December 5). *Introducing Amazon Go and the world's most advanced shopping technology*. Retrieved November 6, 2017, from www.youtube.com/watch?v=NrmMk1Myrxc&t=50s

Amos, J. (2009, October 26). The consequences of dropping out of high school: Average high school dropout has a negative net fiscal contribution to society of $5,200, says new report. *Alliance for Excellent Education*. Retrieved March 1, 2018, from https://all4ed.org/articles/the-consequences-of-dropping-out-of-high-school-average-high-school-dropout-has-a-negative-net-fiscal-contribution-to-society-of-5200-says-new-report

Anderson, J. (2010). *ICT transforming education: A regional guide*. Bangkok, Thailand: UNESCO Bangkok. Retrieved March 1, 2017, from http://unesdoc.unesco.org/images/0018/001892/189216e.pdf

Anderson, L. W., & Krathwohl, D. (Eds.). (2001). *A taxonomy for learning, teaching, and assessing: A revision of Bloom's taxonomy of educational objectives*. Boston: Allyn & Bacon.

Arbesman, S. (2013). *The half-life of facts: Why everything we know has an expiration date*. New York: Current.

Arnett, T. (2016, December 7). *Teaching in the machine age: How innovation can make bad teachers good and good teachers better*. Retrieved March 3, 2018, from https://www.christenseninstitute.org/publications/teaching-machine-age

Artificial intelligence: Anything you can do, AI can do better. So how will it change the workplace? (2016, August 14). *Economist*. Retrieved October 1, 2016, from https://learnmore.economist.com/story/57a849c338ba0ee26d98a68d

Associated Press. (2008, April 1). High school graduation rates plummet below 50 percent in some U.S. cities. *Fox News*. Retrieved March 1, 2018, from www.foxnews.com/story/2008/04/01/high-school-graduation-rates-plummet-below-50-percent-in-some-us-cities.html

AZQuotes. (n.d.). *Mark Strand quotes*. Retrieved January 20, 2017, from www.azquotes.com/author/14217-Mark_Strand

Baldwin, H. (2012, July 24). *Time off to innovate: Good idea or a waste of tech talent?* Retrieved September 20, 2016, from www.computerworld.com/article/2506129/it-management/time-off-to-innovate-good-idea-or-a-waste-of-tech-talent-.html

Ballard, S. (2016, August 8). Why is change so hard? *Psychology Today*. Retrieved March 1, 2018, from https://www.psychologytoday.com/blog/the-truth-about-exercise-addiction/201608/why-is-change-so-hard

Basulto, D. (n.d.). *Why Ray Kurzweil's predictions are right 86% of the time*. Retrieved September 20, 2016, from http://bigthink.com/endless-innovation/why-ray-kurzweils-predictions-are-right-86-of-the-time

Bazelon, E. (2012, August 21). *Benefits of delayed gratification in children*. Retrieved March 1, 2018, from http://health.heraldtribune.com/2012/08/21/benefits-of-delayed-gratification-in-children

Becker, S. A., Freeman, A., Hall, C. G., Cummins, M., & Yuhnke, B. (2016). *NMC/CoSN horizon report: 2016* (K–12 ed.). Austin, TX: New Media Consortium.

Bernard, S. (2010). Neuro myths: Separating fact and fiction in brain-based learning. *Edutopia*. Retrieved March 1, 2018, from www.edutopia.org/neuroscience-brain-based-learning-myth-busting

Bianculli, A. (2001). *Trains and technology: The American railroad in the nineteenth century—Volume 1: Locomotives*. Newark: University of Delaware Press.

Bianculli, A. (2003). *Trains and technology: The American railroad in the nineteenth century—Volume 3: Track and structure*. Newark: University of Delaware Press.

Blanton, A., & Rosenbaum, E. (2013, January 4). *The banana interface*. Retrieved October 1, 2016, from http://makezine.com/projects/make-33/the-banana-interface

Bloom, P. (2013, January). Coming soon: Computers will use the five senses to enhance our lives. *WIRED*. Retrieved March 1, 2018, from www.wired.com/insights/2013/01/coming-soon-computers-will-use-the-five-senses-to-enhance-our-lives

boyd, d. (2014). *It's complicated: The social lives of networked teens*. New Haven, CT: Yale University Press.

Bradley, S. (2015, April 29). Design principles: Compositional flow and rhythm. *Smashing Magazine*. Retrieved March 1, 2018, from www.smashingmagazine.com/2015/04/design-principles-compositional-flow-and-rhythm

Brandt, R. (1988, February). *On changing secondary schools: A conversation with Ted Sizer*. Alexandria, VA: Association for Supervision and Curriculum Development. Retrieved September 1, 2016, from www.ascd.org/ASCD/pdf/journals/ed_lead/el_198802_brandt.pdf

Briggs, S. (2016, May 19). *12 facets of education that will be obsolete by 2025*. Retrieved May 1, 2017, from www.opencolleges.edu.au/informed/features/25-things-that-will-be-obsolete-by-2025

Brighterion. (2017). *Next generation, artificial intelligence and machine learning*. Retrieved March 1, 2018, from https://brighterion.com/next-generation-artificial-intelligence-machine-learning

Bronson, P., & Merryman, A. (2010). The creativity crisis. *Newsweek*. Retrieved March 1, 2018, from www.newsweek.com/creativity-crisis-74665

Brooks, D. (2008, May 2). The cognitive age. *New York Times*. Retrieved June 1, 2017, from www.nytimes.com/2008/05/02/opinion/02brooks.html

Brown, G. C. (2016, April 13). *By 2020 5 million white collar office jobs will disappear*. Retrieved September 20, 2016, from www.linkedin.com/pulse/2020-5-million-white-collar-office-jobs-disappear-world-gary-brown

Brown, M. (2013, May 16). *The value of strategic thinking exercises*. Retrieved September 20, 2016, from http://brainzooming.com/strategic-thinking-exercises-more-than-200-strategic-planning-questions/17443

Bureau of Labor Statistics. (2016, September 22). *Employee tenure summary*. Retrieved January 20, 2017, from www.bls.gov/news.release/tenure.nr0.htm

Burmark, L. (2002). *Visual literacy: Learn to see, see to learn*. Alexandria, VA: Association for Supervision and Curriculum Development.

Cababa, S. (2015). *Tech trends 2015*. Retrieved November 20, 2011, from www.frogdesign.com/html/techtrends2015/index.html

Camera, L. (2015, November 10). Fewer students dropping out of high school. *U.S. News and World Report*. Retrieved December 15, 2016, from www.usnews.com/news/articles/2015/11/10/high-school-dropout-rates-plummet

Canton, J. (2016). *Future smart: Managing the game-changing trends that will transform your world*. Boston: Da Capo Press.

Carr, N. (2010). *The shallows: What the Internet is doing to our brains*. New York: Norton.

Carter, D. (2016, July 6). *Goodbye, linear factory model of schooling: Why learning is irregular*. Retrieved September 20, 2016, from www.edsurge.com/news/2016-07-06-goodbye-linear-factory-model-of-schooling-why-learning-is-irregular

Carter, N. (2014, August 4). *Genius hour and the 6 essentials of personalized education*. Retrieved March 29, 2018, from https://www.edutopia.org/blog/genius-hour-essentials-personalized-education-nichole-carter

Center for Applied Special Technology. (2011). *Universal Design for Learning guidelines version 2.0*. Wakefield, MA: Author.

Christensen, C. M., Horn, M. B., & Johnson, C. W. (2008). *Disrupting class: How disruptive innovation will change the way the world learns*. New York: McGraw-Hill.

Cohen, M. T. (2008, October 23). *The effect of direct instruction versus discovery learning on the understanding of science lessons by second grade students*. Retrieved March 1, 2017, from http://digitalcommons.uconn.edu/cgi/viewcontent.cgi?article=1027&context=nera_2008

Collaborative planning: Integrating curricula across subjects. (2016, April 19). *Edutopia*. Retrieved June 1, 2017, from www.edutopia.org/practice/collaborative-planning-integrating-curricula-across-subjects

Collins, S. (2008). *The hunger games*. New York: Scholastic Press.

Cossie, D. (2010, July 1). *The only thing worse than being blind is having sight but no vision*. Retrieved June 1, 2017, from www.betternetworker.com/articles/

view/personal-development/mindset/the-only-thing-worse-than-being-blind-is-having-sight-but-no-vision

Costa, A. L., & Kallick, B. (Eds.). (2008). *Learning and leading with habits of mind: 16 essential characteristics for success*. Alexandria, VA: Association for Supervision and Curriculum Development.

Costandi, M. (2016). *Neuroplasticity*. Cambridge: MIT Press.

Coughlan, S. (2013, May 8). *Lack of sleep blights pupils' education*. Retrieved September 20, 2016, from www.bbc.com/news/business-22209818

Cramond, B., & Kim, K. (2002). *EPSY 7060 Assessment of Gifted Children and Youth*. https://web.archive.org/web/20080119015727/http:/kyunghee.myweb.uga.edu/portfolio/review%20of%20ttct.htm

Dale, N. (2016, November 16). *How to find the middle ground between data-driven and student-driven learning in your classroom*. Retrieved June 1, 2017, from www.edsurge.com/news/2016-11-16-how-to-find-the-middle-ground-between-data-driven-and-student-driven-learning-in-your-classroom

Davis, J. (2013, October 15). A radical way of unleashing a generation of geniuses. *Wired*. Retrieved September 20, 2016, from www.wired.com/2013/10/free-thinkers

The decline of creativity in the United States: 5 questions for educational psychologist Kyung Hee Kim. (2010, October 18). *Britannica*. Retrieved June 1, 2017, from http://blogs.britannica.com/2010/10/the-decline-of-creativity-in-the-united-states-5-questions-for-educational-psychologist-kyung-hee-kim

Diamandis, P. (2015, October 12). *Ray Kurzweil's wildest prediction: Nanobots will plug our brains into the web by the 2030s*. Retrieved June 1, 2017, from http://singularityhub.com/2015/10/12/ray-kurzweils-wildest-prediction-nanobots-will-plug-our-brains-into-the-web-by-the-2030s

Diamandis, P. H., & Kotler, S. (2012a). *Abundance: The future is better than you think* [Audiobook]. Old Saybrook, CT: Tantor Audio.

Diamandis, P. H., & Kotler, S. (2012b). *Abundance: The future is better than you think*. New York: Free Press.

Dillon, S. (2009, April 22). Large urban-suburban gap seen in graduation rates. *New York Times*. Retrieved September 20, 2016, from www.nytimes.com/2009/04/22/education/22dropout.html

Dimitri, C., Effland, A., & Conklin, N. (2005, June). *The 20th century transformation of U.S. agriculture and farm policy* (Economic Information Bulletin No. 3). Washington, DC: U.S. Department of Agriculture. Retrieved November 2, 2017, from www.ers.usda.gov/webdocs/publications/44197/13566_eib3_1_.pdf

Dobbs, R., Madgavkar, A., Barton, D., Labaye, E., Manyika, J., Roxburgh, C., Lund, S., & Madhav, S. (2012, June). *The world at work: Jobs, pay, and skills for 3.5 billion people*. Retrieved March 1, 2018, from www.mckinsey.com/global-themes/employment-and-growth/the-world-at-work

Dodge, B. (1995). *Some thoughts about WebQuests*. Retrieved December 12, 2017, from http://webquest.org/sdsu/about_webquests.html

Doidge, N. (2007). *The brain that changes itself: Stories of personal triumph from the frontiers of brain science*. New York: Viking.

Domoff, S. E., Harrison, K., Gearhardt, A. N., Gentile, D. A., Lumeng, J. C., & Miller, A. L. (2017, November 16). Development and validation of the problematic media use measure: A parent report measure of screen media "addiction" in children. *Psychology of Popular Media Culture*. Retrieved March 12, 2018, from http://dx.doi.org/10.1037/ppm0000163

Donchev, D. (2017, July 29). *36 mind blowing YouTube facts, figures and statistics—2017*. Retrieved November 2, 2017, from https://fortunelords.com/youtube-statistics

Dorrier, J. (2015, April 20). *Looking ahead as Moore's law turns 50: What's next for computing?* Retrieved June 1, 2017, from http://singularityhub.com/2015/04/20/looking-ahead-as-moores-law-turns-50-whats-next-for-computing

Doyle, A. (2017, May 1). *How often do people change jobs?* Retrieved November 2, 2017, from www.thebalance.com/how-often-do-people-change-jobs-2060467

Durden, T. (2017, February 13). *Goldman had 600 cash equity traders in 2000; it now has 2*. Retrieved November 2, 2017, from www.zerohedge.com/news/2017-02-13/goldman-had-600-cash-equity-traders-2000-it-now-has-2

Dweck, C. (2016, January 13). What having a "growth mindset" actually means. *Harvard Business Review*. Retrieved June 1, 2017, from https://hbr.org/2016/01/what-having-a-growth-mindset-actually-means

Dyer, K. (2016, May 24). *Take three!: 55 digital tools and apps for formative assessment success*. Retrieved June 1, 2017, from www.nwea.org/blog/2016/take-three-55-digital-tools-and-apps-for-formative-assessment-success

Eadicicco, L. (2015, December 15). Americans check their phones 8 billion times a day. *Time*. Retrieved September 25, 2016, from http://time.com/4147614/smartphone-usage-us-2015

EdSurge. (2016, April 6). *Survey: 50% of educators bring games into classroom; request better dashboards and reports*. Retrieved October 10, 2016, from www.edsurge.com/news/2016-04-06-survey-50-of-educators-bring-games-into-classroom-request-better-dashboards-and-reports

Einstein, A., & Calaprice, A. (2013). *The ultimate quotable Einstein*. Princeton, NJ: Princeton University Press.

Ekebipop, A. (2016, February 27). *Fast industrial robot production line in Europe*. Retrieved November 6, 2017, from www.youtube.com/watch?v=884ZjrTErcM

The elephant in the truck: Retraining low-skilled workers. (2017, January 12). *Economist*. Retrieved June 1, 2017, from www.economist.com/news/special-report/21714175-systems-continuous-reskilling-threaten-buttress-inequality-retraining-low-skilled

Elmore, R. (2006). *Education leadership as the practice of improvement* [Audio recording]. Retrieved October 3, 2016, from www.scottmcleod.org/2006UCEAElmore.mp3

Equitas. (2016). *Welcome to the exponential age: The new industrial revolution*. Retrieved June 1, 2017, from www.equitas-capital.com/2016/research/welcome-to-the-exponential-age-the-new-industrial-revolution

Ferlazzo, L. (2013, March 3). *The best resources for learning about the concept of "transfer"—Help me find more*. Retrieved June 1, 2017, from http://larryferlazzo.edublogs.org/2013/03/03/the-best-resources-for-learning-about-the-concept-of-transfer-help-me-find-more

Ferlazzo, L. (2015, January 16). *The best resources about inductive learning and teaching*. Retrieved June 1, 2017, from http://larryferlazzo.edublogs.org/2015/01/16/the-best-resources-about-inductive-learning-teaching

Flipped Learning Network. (2016). *What is flipped learning?* Retrieved June 1, 2017, from https://flippedlearning.org/wp-content/uploads/2016/07/FLIP_handout_FNL_Web.pdf

Florida, R. (2014). *The rise of the creative class revisited*. New York: Basic Books.

Fractus Learning. (n.d.). *Bloom's taxonomy verbs*. Retrieved June 1, 2017, from https://fractuslearning.com/wp-content/uploads/2016/01/blooms-taxonomy-verbs.png

Freeman, A., Becker, S. A., Cummins, M., Davis, A., & Giesinger, C. H. (2017). *NMC/CoSN horizon report: 2017* (K–12 ed.). Austin, TX: New Media Consortium.

Frey, T. (2011, November 11). *55 jobs of the future*. Retrieved December 15, 2016, from www.futuristspeaker.com/business-trends/55-jobs-of-the-future

Friedman, T. L. (2006). *The world is flat: A brief history of the twenty-first century*. New York: Farrar, Straus and Giroux.

Friedman, T. L. (2016a). *Thank you for being late: An optimist's guide to thriving in the age of accelerations* [Audiobook]. New York: Macmillan Audio.

Friedman, T. L. (2016b). *Thank you for being late: An optimist's guide to thriving in the age of accelerations*. New York: Farrar, Straus and Giroux.

Garner, M. (2015). Finland schools: Subjects scrapped and replaced with "topics" as country reforms its education system. *Independent*. Retrieved March 1, 2018, from www.independent.co.uk/news/world/europe/finland-schools-subjects-are-out-and-topics-are-in-as-country-reforms-its-education-system-10123911.html

Generation uphill. (2016, January 23). *Economist*. Retrieved September 30, 2016, from www.economist.com/news/special-report/21688591-millennials-are-brainiest-best-educated-generation-ever-yet-their-elders-often

Ghogomu, M. (2014, June 18). *70% of young children can use a computer mouse. Only 11% can tie their own shoes* [Infographic]. Retrieved September 26, 2016, from http://thehigherlearning.com/2014/06/18/70-of-young-children-can-use-a-computer-mouse-only-11-can-tie-their-own-shoes-infographic

Gillard, J. (2011). Julia Gillard's speech to Congress. *Sydney Morning Herald*. Retrieved from https://www.smh.com.au/world/julia-gillards-speech-to-congress-20110310-1boee.html

Glatter, H., Deruy, E., & Wong, A. (2016, August 26). Fixing America's broken school calendar. *The Atlantic*. Retrieved March 1, 2018, from https://www.theatlantic.com/education/archive/2016/08/education-eden-the-calendar/497687

The Glossary of Education Reform. (2015). *Personalized learning*. Retrieved March 1, 2018, from www.edglossary.org/personalized-learning

Goodman, S. (2014, March 18). *Fuel creativity in the classroom with divergent thinking*. Retrieved June 1, 2017, from www.edutopia.org/blog/fueling-creativity-through-divergent-thinking-classroom-stacey-goodman

Gould, S., & Weller, C. (2015, October 1). Most common reasons students drop out of high school are heartbreaking. *Business Insider*. Retrieved December 15, 2016, from www.businessinsider.com/most-common-reasons-students-drop-out-of-high-school-2015-10

Greene, K. (2016a, October 11). *How cross-curricular lessons inspire critical thinking*. Retrieved November 1, 2017, from https://edtechdigest.wordpress.com/2016/10/11/how-cross-curricular-lessons-inspire-critical-thinking

Greene, K. (2016b, October 25). *Why every class should be cross-curricular*. Retrieved June 1, 2017, from www.eschoolnews.com/2016/10/25/why-every-class-should-be-cross-curricular

Grossman, L. (2011, February 10). 2045: The year man becomes mortal. *TIME*. Retrieved March 1, 2018, from http://content.time.com/time/magazine/article/0,9171,2048299,00.html

Hawkins, B., & Oblinge, D. (2006). The myth of the digital divide. *EDUCAUSE Review*, *41*(4), 12–13.

Haynes, K. (2015). *Top 12 ways to bring the real world into your classroom*. Retrieved June 1, 2017, from www.teachhub.com/top-12-ways-bring-real-world-your-classroom

Heick, T. (2014). *Evolve or be replaced: 12 emerging realities teachers must adapt to* [Blog post]. Retrieved November 11, 2017, from www.teachthought.com/the-future-of-learning/disrupting-education-8-ideas-will-break

Heick, T. (2018, November 5). *How Google impacts the way students think*. [Blog post.] Retrieved March 11, 2018, from www.teachthought.com/critical-thinking/how-google-impacts-the-way-students-think

Heid, M. (2011, August 2). This is your brain on exercise. *Men's Health*. Retrieved June 1, 2017, from www.menshealth.com/fitness/this-is-your-brain-on-exercise

Hendry, E. (2013). *7 epic fails brought to you by the genius mind of Thomas Edison*. Retrieved March 7, 2018, from https://www.smithsonianmag.com/innovation/7-epic-fails-brought-to-you-by-the-genius-mind-of-thomas-edison-180947786

Hindle, T. (2009). Just-in-time. *Economist*. Retrieved March 1, 2018, from www.economist.com/node/13976392

Holland, B. (2017, May 17). *Teaching 21st century skills requires more than just technology*. Retrieved June 1, 2017, from http://blogs.edweek.org/edweek/edtechresearcher/2017/05/teaching_21st_century_skills_requires_more_than_just_technology.html

Hoque, F. (2015). How the rising gig economy is reshaping businesses. *Fast Company*. Retrieved March 1, 2018, from www.fastcompany.com/3051315/the-gig-economy-is-going-global-heres-why-and-what-it-means

Hreha, J. (2017). Instant gratification is good for you: Lessons for education. *Big Think*. Retrieved March 1, 2018, from http://bigthink.com/wikimind/instant-gratification-is-good-for-you-lessons-for-education

HRreview. (2013). *UK workers specialist skills are under threat*. Retrieved from http://www.hrreview.co.uk/hr-news/strategy-news/uk-workers-specialist-skills-are-under-threat/49215

Hubbard, https://quoteinvestigator.com/2015/01/26/doing/

Ice bucket challenge. (n.d.). In *Wikipedia*. Retrieved December 12, 2017, from https://en.wikipedia.org/wiki/Ice_Bucket_Challenge

Integrated learning: One project, several disciplines. (2015, May 20). Retrieved June 1, 2017, from www.edutopia.org/practice/integrated-learning-one-project-several-disciplines

James, J. (1997). *Thinking in the future tense: A workout for the mind*. New York: Free Press.

Jensen, E. (2008). *Brain-based learning: The new paradigm of teaching* (2nd ed.). Thousand Oaks, CA: Corwin.

Johnson, B. (2013, January 15). *Deeper learning: Why cross-curricular teaching is essential*. Retrieved June 1, 2017, from www.edutopia.org/blog/cross-curricular-teaching-deeper-learning-ben-johnson

Jukes, I. (2017). *A brief introduction to the eight I's of modern learning*. Unpublished learning materials for the Texas Academy of Leadership in the Humanities, Lamar University, Beaumont, TX.

Jukes, I., Dosaj, A., Matheson, K., McKay, B., McKay, W., Holmes, L., et al. (1999). *NetSavvy: Information literacy for the communication age*. Washington, DC: International Society for Technology in Education.

Jukes, I., & McCain, T. (2005). *New schools for a new millennium*. Retrieved August 1, 2016, from ww3.templejc.edu/prodev/distance-ed/fusion2009/ian-jukes.pdf

Jukes, I., McCain, T., & Crockett, L. (2010). *Understanding the digital generation: Teaching and learning in the new digital landscape*. Thousand Oaks, CA: Corwin.

Jukes, I., Schaaf, R. L., & Mohan, N. (2015). *Reinventing learning for the always-on generation: Strategies and apps that work*. Bloomington, IN: Solution Tree Press.

Keeping an eye on Google—Eye tracking SERPs through the years. (n.d.). *Mediative*. Retrieved March 1, 2018, from www.mediative.com/eye-tracking-google-through-the-years

Kim, K. (2002). *Critique on the Torrance Tests of Creative Thinking*. Retrieved from https://web.archive.org/web/20080119015727/http:/kyunghee.myweb.uga.edu/portfolio/review%20of%20ttct.htm

Klemm, W. (2014). Memory gimmicks 4: Story chains. *Psychology Today*. Retrieved March 1, 2018, from www.psychologytoday.com/blog/memory-medic/201409/memory-gimmicks-4-story-chains

Kohn, A. (2001). *One-size-fits-all education doesn't work*. Retrieved March 1, 2018, from www.alfiekohn.org/article/one-size-fits-education-doesnt-work

Kolb, B., Gibb, R., & Robinson, T. (1998). *Brain plasticity and behavior*. Lethbridge, Alberta: Canadian Centre for Behavioural Neuroscience. Retrieved September 30, 2016, from www.psychologicalscience.org/journals/cd/12_1/kolb.cfm

Konnikova, M. (2014). Being a better online reader. *The New Yorker*. Retrieved March 1, 2018, from www.newyorker.com/science/maria-konnikova/being-a-better-online-reader

Land, G. T., & Jarman, B. (2000). *Breakpoint and beyond: Mastering the future—today*. Champaign, IL: HarperBusiness.

Lapidos, J. (2007, July 11). Do kids need a summer vacation? *Slate*. Retrieved September 20, 2016, from www.slate.com/articles/news_and_politics/explainer/2007/07/do_kids_need_a_summer_vacation.html

Larson, J., & Micheels-Cyrus, M. (1986). *Seeds of peace: A catalogue of quotations*. Vancouver, British Columbia, Canada: New Society.

Learning and earning: Lifelong learning is becoming an economic imperative. (2017, January 12). *Economist*. Retrieved November 7, 2017, from www.economist.com/news/special-report/21714169-technological-change-demands-stronger-and-more-continuous-connections-between-education

Lehmann, C. (2011, November 3). *ISTE keynote presentation*. Retrieved March 1, 2018, from www.youtube.com/watch?v=3xgawG-yCew

Lengel, J. (2012). *Education 3.0: Seven steps to better schools*. New York: Teachers College Press.

Levy, F., & Murnane, R. (2013, July 17). *Dancing with robots: Human skills for computerized work*. Retrieved March 1, 2018, from www.thirdway.org/report/dancing-with-robots-human-skills-for-computerized-work

Levinson, M. (2016, January 21). *Transdisciplinarity: Thinking inside and outside the box*. Retrieved June 1, 2017, from www.edutopia.org/blog/transdiciplinarity-thinking-inside-outside-box-matt-levinson

Lombardi, M. A. (2007, March 5). Why is a minute divided into 60 seconds, an hour into 60 minutes, yet there are only 24 hours in a day? *Scientific American*. Retrieved September 20, 2016, from www.scientificamerican.com/article/experts-time-division-days-hours-minutes

Long, H. (2016, March 29). *U.S. has lost 5 million manufacturing jobs since 2000*. Retrieved September 20, 2016, from http://money.cnn.com/2016/03/29/news/economy/us-manufacturing-jobs

Macey, T. (2017, July 14). *7 best practices for implementing just-in-time learning* [Blog post]. Retrieved March 1, 2018, from www.advantageperformance.com/implementing-just-in-time-learning

MacQuarrie, B. (2013). Malala Yousafzai addresses Harvard audience. *Boston Globe*. Retrieved from https://www.bostonglobe.com/metro/2013/09/27/malala-yousafzai-pakistani-teen-shot-taliban-tells-harvard-audience-that-education-right-for-all/6cZBan0M4J3cAnmRZLfUmI/story.html

Mansilla, V. B., & Jackson, A. (2011). *Educating for global competence: Preparing our youth to engage the world*. Retrieved June 1, 2017, from http://asiasociety.org/files/book-globalcompetence.pdf

Manyika, J., Chui, M., Miremadi, M., Bughin, J., George, K., Willmott, P., & Dewhurst, M. (2017, January). *Harnessing automation for a future that works*. Retrieved from https://www.mckinsey.com/global-themes/digital-disruption/harnessing-automation-for-a-future-that-works

Markman, A. (n.d.). *Picasso, Kepler, and the benefits of being an expert generalist*. Retrieved June 1, 2017, from http://99u.com/articles/7269/picasso-kepler-and-the-benefits-of-being-an-expert-generalist

Martin, K. (2017, May 26). *Rethinking the lesson plan*. Retrieved June 1, 2017, from https://katielmartin.com/2017/05/26/rethinking-the-lesson-plan

Martin, P. (2016, August 19). *We're moving part-time as the jobs market hollows out*. Retrieved September 25, 2016, from www.petermartin.com.au/2016/08/were-moving-part-time-as-jobs-market.html

Martinez, S. L., & Stager, G. S. (2013, November 5). *The ultimate guide to bringing the maker movement to your classroom*. Retrieved September 20, 2016, from www.weareteachers.com/making-matters-how-the-maker-movement-is-transforming-education

Marvin, N. (Producer), & Darabont, F. (Writer/
Director). (1994). *The Shawshank redemption*
[Motion picture]. United States: Columbia
Pictures and Castle Rock Entertainment.

Masser, M., & Creed, L. (1985). Greatest love of all
[Recorded by W. Houston]. On *Whitney Houston*.
New York: Sony.

McCain, T. (2005). *Teaching for tomorrow: Teaching
content and problem-solving skills*. Thousand Oaks,
CA: Corwin.

McCain, T., & Jukes, I. (2000). *Windows on the future:
Education in the age of technology*. Thousand Oaks,
CA: Corwin.

McCain, T., & Jukes, I. (2007). *Windows on the
future: Thinking about tomorrow today*. Retrieved
August 1, 2016, from http://wvde.state.wv.us/
principalsinstitute/institute07-08/docs_summer/
SummerDay04_Jukes—WindowsOnTheFuture.pdf

McCain, T., Jukes, I., & Crockett, L. (2010). *Living
on the future edge: Windows on tomorrow*. Kelowna,
BC, Canada: 21st Century Fluency Project.

McCarthy, J. (2015, December 3). *Authenticity = lifelong
learners*. Retrieved June 1, 2017, from www
.edutopia.org/blog/authenticity-equals-lifelong-
learners-john-mccarthy

Mead, M. (2005). *The world ahead: An anthropologist
anticipates the future*. New York: Berghahn Books.

Medina, J. (2008). *Brain rules: 12 principles for surviving
and thriving at work, home, and school*. Seattle, WA:
Pear Press.

Meltzer, T. (2014, June 15). Robot doctors, online
lawyers and automated architects: The future
of the professions? *Guardian*. Retrieved
September 30, 2016, from www.theguardian.com/
technology/2014/jun/15/robot-doctors-online-
lawyers-automated-architects-future-professions-
jobs-technology

Miller, A. (2017). A more complete picture
of student learning. *Edutopia*. Retrieved
from https://www.edutopia.org/article/
more-complete-picture-student-learning

Mind Blowing Videos. (2016, July 26). *Amazon
warehouse robots*. Retrieved from https://www
.youtube.com/watch?v=cLVCGEmkJs0

Mikkelson, B. (2005, November 3). *Grandma's cooking
secret*. Retrieved September 20, 2016, from www
.snopes.com/weddings/newlywed/secret.asp

Mogg, T. (2012, November 12). *Apple introduces "blue
sky" program to give select employees time for personal
projects*. Retrieved September 22, 2016, from www
.digitaltrends.com/apple/apple-introduces-blue-
sky-program-to-give-select-employees-time-for-
personal-projects

Monson, T. S. (2003). *In search of treasure*. https://
www.lds.org/general-conference/2003/04/
in-search-of-treasure?lang=eng

Moore, C. (2010, September). Buckets and fires.
Educational Leadership, 68(1). Retrieved September
20, 2017, from www.ascd.org/publications/
educational-leadership/sept10/vol68/num01/
Buckets-and-Fires.aspx

Morgan, J. (2016, February 11). The lab, the factory
and the future of work. *Forbes*. Retrieved
March 1, 2016, from www.forbes.com/sites/
jacobmorgan/2016/02/11/lab-factory-future-
work

Morrison, K. (2015, July 2). Visual media changes how
humans consume information. *Adweek*. Retrieved
March 1, 2018, from www.adweek.com/digital/
visual-media-webdam-infographic

Mulcahey, D. (2016, October 27). Who wins
in the gig economy, and who loses.
Harvard Business Review. Retrieved March
1, 2018, from https://hbr.org/2016/10/
who-wins-in-the-gig-economy-and-who-loses

Murray, J. (2015, June 30). *How to build your
PLN*. Retrieved June 1, 2017, from http://
askatechteacher.com/2015/06/30/
how-to-build-your-pln

Murray, P., & Gillibrand, K. (2015, April 20).
*Contingent workforce: Size, characteristics, earnings,
and benefits*. Retrieved September 23, 2016, from
www.gao.gov/assets/670/669899.pdf

National Education Association of the United
States. (1894). *Report of The Committee of Ten
on secondary school studies*. Retrieved March
5, 2018, from https://archive.org/details/
reportofcomtens00natirich

Neisser, U. (1997). Rising scores on intelligence tests.
American Scientist, 85, 440–447.

New Media Consortium (n.d.). *The horizon reports*.
Retrieved September 20, 2016, from www.nmc
.org/publication-type/horizon-report

O'Connor, S. (2017). Driven to despair—the hidden
costs of the gig economy. *Financial Times*.
Retrieved March 1, 2018, from www.ft.com/
content/749cb87e-6ca8-11e7-b9c7-15af748b60d0

Old dogs, new tricks: How older employees perform
in the workplace. (2017, January 12). *Economist*.
Retrieved June 1, 2017, from www.economist
.com/news/special-report/21714174-people-age-
brain-changes-both-good-ways-and-bad-how-
older-employees-perform

Outsource2India. (2016). *Healthcare BPO*. Retrieved
November 1, 2017, from www.outsource2india
.com/Healthcare/medical-imaging-services.asp

Padnani, A. (2012, August 11). The power of music, tapped in a cubicle. *New York Times*. Retrieved June 1, 2017, from www.nytimes.com/2012/08/12/jobs/how-music-can-improve-worker-productivity-workstation.html

Palmer, A. (2017, January 12). Learning and earning: Lifelong learning is becoming an economic imperative. *Economist*. Retrieved June 1, 2017, from www.economist.com/news/special-report/21714169-technological-change-demands-stronger-and-more-continuous-connections-between-education

Pappas, C. (2016, December 17). *5 tips to integrate discovery learning activities into your instructional design*. Retrieved June 1, 2017, from https://elearningindustry.com/tips-integrate-discovery-learning-activities-instructional-design

Partnership for 21st Century Learning. (n.d.). What we know about critical thinking. *The 4Cs Research Series*. Retrieved March 1, 2018, from www.p21.org/storage/documents/docs/Research/P21_4Cs_Research_Brief_Series_-_Critical_Thinking.pdf

Patkar, M. (2014, July 22). *Learn the basics of color theory to know what looks good*. Retrieved June 1, 2017, from http://lifehacker.com/learn-the-basics-of-color-theory-to-know-what-looks-goo-1608972072

Petriglieri, G., Ashford, S., & Wrzesniewski, A. (2018). Thriving in the gig economy. *Harvard Business Review*. Retrieved March 1, 2018, from https://hbr.org/2018/03/thriving-in-the-gig-economy

Pfeffer, J. (2015, July 30). *The case against the "gig economy."* Retrieved September 28, 2016, from http://fortune.com/2015/07/30/freelance-vs-full-time-employees

Pink, D. H. (2001, October). *School's out: Get ready for the new age of individualized education*. Retrieved September 26, 2016, from http://reason.com/archives/2001/10/01/schools-out

Pink, D. H. (2006). *A whole new mind: Why right-brainers will rule the future*. New York: Penguin.

Poe, E. A. (1982). The tell-tale heart. In *The tell-tale heart and other writings by Edgar Allan Poe*. New York: Bantam. (Originally published in 1843.)

PricewaterhouseCoopers. (2015, April). *A smart move*. Retrieved September 20, 2016, from https://pwc.docalytics.com/v/a-smart-move-pwc-stem-report-april-2015.pdf

Proust, M. (n.d.) In *Wikiquote*. Retrieved March 30, 2018, from https://en.wikiquote.org/wiki/Marcel_Proust

Quillen, I. (2013, April 25). *A design challenge to students: Solve a real-world problem!* Retrieved November 1, 2017, from ww2.kqed.org/mindshift/2013/04/25/a-design-challenge-to-students-solve-a-real-world-problem

Rankin, W. (2011, June 1). *Teaching and learning in the 3rd information age*. Retrieved January 15, 2017, from https://itunes.apple.com/us/itunes-u/ade-keynotes/id441669904?mt=10

Ratey, J. J. (2013). *Spark: The revolutionary new science of exercise and the brain*. New York: Little, Brown.

Real-world problem solving: Project-based solutions. (2015, November 10). Retrieved June 1, 2017, from www.edutopia.org/practice/real-world-problem-solving-project-based-solutions

Rejcek, P. (2017, March 31). *Can futurists predict the year of the singularity?* Retrieved March 5, 2018, from https://singularityhub.com/2017/03/31/can-futurists-predict-the-year-of-the-singularity

Richardson, W., & Dixon, B. (2017). *10 principles for schools of modern learning*. [White paper]. Retrieved from https://s3-us-west-2.amazonaws.com/modernlearners/Modern+Learners+10+Principles+for+Schools+of+Modern+Learning+whitepaper.pdf

Rivero, L. (2012, March 10). Be more creative today. *Psychology Today*. Retrieved June 1, 2017, from www.psychologytoday.com/blog/creative-synthesis/201203/be-more-creative-today

Rothstein, D., & Santana, L. (2011). *Make just one change: Teach students to ask their own questions*. Cambridge, MA: Harvard Education Press.

Rotman, D. (2017, February 13). *The relentless pace of automation*. Retrieved November 1, 2017, from www.technologyreview.com/s/603465/the-relentless-pace-of-automation

St. Fleur, N. (2017). How whales became the biggest animals on the planet. *New York Times*. Retrieved March 1, 2018, from www.nytimes.com/2017/05/24/science/whales-evolution-oceans.html

Samantha. (2012, January 7). *The origin of the QWERTY keyboard*. Retrieved September 20, 2016, from www.todayifoundout.com/index.php/2012/01/the-origin-of-the-qwerty-keyboard

Satel, G. (2015, February 6). Why communication is today's most important skill. *Forbes*. Retrieved March 1, 2018, from www.forbes.com/sites/gregsatell/2015/02/06/why-communication-is-todays-most-important-skill

Scenario-Based Learning. (n.d.). *Massey University*. Retrieved March 29, 2018, from www.massey.ac.nz/massey/fms/AVC%20Academic/Teaching%20and%20Learning%20Cenrtres/Scenario-based-learning.pdf

Schaaf, R. (2014a). Cyberbullying: Policy for digital protection. *New Horizons for Learning, 11*(1). Retrieved March 1, 2018, from http://jhepp .library.jhu.edu/ojs/index.php/newhorizons/ article/view/349/158

Schaaf, R. (2014b). *100 things students can create to demonstrate what they know*. Retrieved June 1, 2017, from www.teachthought.com/pedagogy/ assessment/60-things-students-can-create-to-demonstrate-what-they-know

Schwartz, K. (2015, July 15). *Making learning visible: Doodling helps memories stick*. Retrieved September 30, 2016, from ww2.kqed.org/ mindshift/2015/07/15/making-learning-visible-doodling-helps-memories-stick

Schwartz, K. (2017, April 26). *The essential underpinnings of shifting to "modern learning."* Retrieved June 1, 2017, from https://ww2 .kqed.org/mindshift/2017/04/26/the-essential-underpinnings-of-shifting-to-modern-learning

Sehgal, E. (1984, October). *Occupational mobility and job tenure in 1983*. Retrieved September 20, 2016, from www.bls.gov/opub/mlr/1984/10/ art2full.pdf

Serial. (n.d.). In *Wikipedia*. Retrieved March 31, 2017, from https://en.wikipedia.org/wiki/ Serial_(podcast)

Simmons, M. (2017, April 25). *How Elon Musk learns faster and better than everyone else*. Retrieved June 1, 2017, from https://qz.com/968101/how-elon-musk-learns-faster-and-better-than-everyone-else

Small, G., & Vorgan, G. (2008). *iBrain: Surviving the technological alteration of the modern mind*. New York: William Morrow.

Smith, A. (2016, March 10). *Public predictions for the future of workforce automation*. Retrieved September 20, 2016, from www.pewinternet .org/2016/03/10/public-predictions-for-the-future-of-workforce-automation

Smith, A., & Anderson, J. (2014, August 6). *AI, robotics, and the future of jobs*. Retrieved September 20, 2016, from www.pewinternet.org/2014/08/06/ future-of-jobs

Smith, F. (2016, February 25). Report: One in four students enrolled in online courses. *EdTech*. Retrieved March 3, 2018, from https:// edtechmagazine.com/higher/article/2016/02/ report-one-four-students-enrolled-online-courses

Solving real-world issues through problem-based learning. (2016, November 1). Retrieved June 1, 2017, from www.edutopia.org/practice/solving-real-world-issues-through-problem-based-learning

Sousa, D. A. (Ed.). (2010). *Mind, brain, and education: Neuroscience implications for the classroom*. Bloomington, IN: Solution Tree Press.

Stanton, J. (2013, February 1). *The American education system is creating ignorant adults*. Retrieved June 1, 2017, from www.intrepidreport.com/ archives/8884

Statistic Brain. (2016, September 1). *YouTube company statistics*. Retrieved June 1, 2017, from www .statisticbrain.com/youtube-statistics

Steinbeck, J. (1945). *Cannery Row*. New York: Viking.

Stephenson, G. R. (1967). Cultural acquisition of a specific learned response among rhesus monkeys. In D. Starek, R. Schneider, & H. J. Kuhn (Eds.), *Progress in primatology* (pp. 279–288). Stuttgart, Germany: Fischer.

Sternberg, R. J. (1985). *Beyond IQ: A triarchic theory of intelligence*. New York: Cambridge University Press.

Strand, M. (2016). *Collected poems*. New York: Knopf.

Strauss, K. (2017, March 8). 10 great "gig economy" jobs for 2017. *Forbes*. Retrieved March 1, 2018, from https://www.forbes.com/sites/ karstenstrauss/2017/03/08/10-great-gig-economy-jobs-for-2017

Swanson, M. (n.d.). *The Babylonian number system*. Retrieved September 20, 2017, from www.math .ucdenver.edu/~jloats/Student%20pdfs/15_ BabylonianNumbers.pdf

Taylor, F. W. (1910). *The principles of scientific management*. New York: Harper & Bros. 34 strategies for the stages of assessment: Before, during and after. (n.d.). Retrieved June 1, 2017, from www.teachthought.com/pedagogy/ assessment/34-strategies-for-the-stages-of-assessment-before-during-after

Treadwell, M. (2016, March 12). *Do we need to read and write to learn?* Retrieved June 1, 2017, from https://mtreadwell.wordpress.com/2016/03/12/ the-end-of-reading-writing

Uber Advanced Technologies Group. (2016, May 16). *Otto—Self-driving trucks*. Retrieved November 6, 2017, from www.youtube.com/ watch?v=bK76W1kH4JA

U.S. Bureau of Labor Statistics. (2017, October 20). *National longitudinal surveys*. Retrieved November 3, 2017, from www.bls.gov/nls/ nlsfaqs.htm

Vander Ark, C., & Ryerse, M. (2017, January 20). *10 reasons why lifelong learning is the only option*. Retrieved June 1, 2017, from www.gettingsmart .com/2017/01/10-reasons-why-lifelong-learning-is-the-only-option van der Pluijm, R., Simmonds, R., & Holmen, M. (2015, June 10). *Search vs. discovery*. Retrieved November 1, 2017. from https://medium.com/the-graph/search-vs-discovery-1b80e045aea

Van Erp, N., & Fenton, D. (2016, May 12). *Try this, not that: Make over your lessons to promote student understanding and curiosity*. Retrieved June 1, 2017, from http://inservice.ascd.org/try-this-not-that-make-over-your-lessons-to-promote-student-understanding-and-curiosity

velocityglobal. (2017, May 16). *Think global: Benefits of a global workforce*. Retrieved March 1, 2018, from https://velocityglobal.com/blog/benefits-of-a-global-workforce

Vesalainen, T. (2017, March 5). Mindmap, brainstorm, idea, innovation, imagination. Retrieved November 6, 2017, from https://pixabay.com/en/mindmap-brainstorm-idea-innovation-2123973

Voltz, D. L., Sims, M. J., & Nelson, B. (2010). *Connecting teachers, students, and standards: Strategies for success in diverse and inclusive classrooms*. Alexandria, VA: Association for Supervision and Curriculum Development.

Wagner, T. (2010). *The global achievement gap: Why even our best schools don't teach the new survival skills our children need—And what we can do about it*. New York: Basic Books.

Wagner, T., & Dintersmith, T. (2015). *Most likely to succeed: Preparing our kids for the innovation era*. New York: Scribner.

Wallis, C. (2017, May 31). Is the U.S. education system producing a society of "smart fools"? *Scientific American*. Retrieved June 1, 2017, from www.scientificamerican.com/article/is-the-u-s-education-system-producing-a-society-of-ldquo-smart-fools-rdquo

Warlick, D. (2011). *2¢ worth* [Personal blog]. Retrieved September 20, 2016, from http://2cents.onlearning.us/?author=1&paged=186

Watters, A. (2015, April 25). *The invented history of "the factory model of education."* Retrieved September 20, 2016, from http://hackeducation.com/2015/04/25/factory-model

WebQuest. (n.d.). In *Wikipedia*. Retrieved December 12, 2017, from https://en.wikipedia.org/wiki/WebQuest

Weissmann, J. (2012, March 29). Why do so many Americans drop out of college? *Atlantic*. Retrieved September 20, 2016, from www.theatlantic.com/business/archive/2012/03/why-do-so-many-americans-drop-out-of-college/255226

Whale facts. Retrieved March 1, 2018, from www.whalefacts.org/what-do-blue-whales-eat

White, M. (2012, April 18). *Hot teaching trend and Common Core: Discovery learning vs. direct instruction*. Retrieved June 1, 2017, from www.deseretnews.com/article/765569782/Discovery-learning-a-major-national-trend-in-education.html

Whitehead, A. (1967). *Adventures in ideas*. New York: Macmillan.

Wiggins, G. (1993). *Assessing student performance: Exploring the purpose and limits of testing*. San Francisco: Jossey-Bass.

Wiggins, G. (2002, January 21). *Grant Wiggins: Defining assessment*. Retrieved June 1, 2017, from www.edutopia.org/grant-wiggins-assessment

Wiggins, G., & McTighe, J. (2005). *Understanding by design* (2nd expanded ed.). Alexandria, VA: Association for Supervision and Curriculum Development.

Willis, J. (2007, Summer). The neuroscience of joyful education. *Educational Leadership, 64*. Retrieved May 1, 2017, from www.ascd.org/publications/educational-leadership/summer07/vol64/num09/The-Neuroscience-of-Joyful-Education.aspx

Wiseman, L. (2014). *Rookie smarts: Why learning beats knowing in the new game of work*. New York: HarperBusiness.

Woollaston, V. (2015, October 29). How often do YOU check your phone?: Average user picks up their device 85 times a DAY—Twice as often as they realise. *Daily Mail*. Retrieved September 25, 2016, from www.dailymail.co.uk/sciencetech/article-3294994/How-check-phone-Average-user-picks-device-85-times-DAY-twice-realise.html

World Economic Forum. (2015). *New vision for education: Unlocking the potential of technology*. Retrieved June 1, 2017, from www3.weforum.org/docs/WEFUSA_NewVisionforEducation_Report2015.pdf

World Economic Forum. (2016a, January). *The future of jobs: Employment, skills and workforce strategy for the fourth Industrial Revolution*. Retrieved November 1, 2017, from www3.weforum.org/docs/WEF_Future_of_Jobs.pdf

World Economic Forum. (2016b, January). *Skills stability*. Retrieved September 10, 2018, from http://reports.weforum.org/future-of-jobs-2016/skills-stability/

World Economic Forum. (2016c, March). *New vision for education: Fostering social and emotional learning through technology*. Retrieved March 15, 2017, from www3.weforum.org/docs/WEF_New_Vision_for_Education.pdf

Wurman, R. S. (1989). *Information anxiety*. New York: Doubleday.

INDEX

CORWIN LEADERSHIP

Anthony Kim & Alexis Gonzales-Black

Designed to foster flexibility and continuous innovation, this resource expands cutting-edge management and organizational techniques to empower schools with the agility and responsiveness vital to their new environment.

Jonathan Eckert

Explore the collective and reflective approach to progress, process, and programs that will build conditions that lead to strong leadership and teaching, which will improve student outcomes.

PJ Caposey

Offering a fresh perspective on teacher evaluation, this book guides administrators to transform their school culture and evaluation process to improve teacher practice and, ultimately, student achievement.

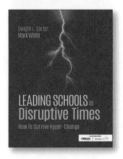

Dwight L. Carter & Mark White

Through understanding the past and envisioning the future, the authors use practical exercises and real-life examples to draw the blueprint for adapting schools to the age of hyper-change.

Raymond L. Smith & Julie R. Smith

This solid, sustainable, and laser-sharp focus on instructional leadership strategies for coaching might just be your most impactful investment toward student achievement.

Simon T. Bailey & Marceta F. Reilly

This engaging resource provides a simple, sustainable framework that will help you move your school from mediocrity to brilliance.

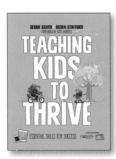

Debbie Silver & Dedra Stafford

Equip educators to develop resilient and mindful learners primed for academic growth and personal success.

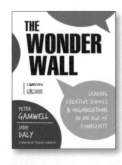

Peter Gamwell & Jane Daly

Discover a new perspective on how to nurture creativity, innovation, leadership, and engagement.

Leadership That Makes an Impact

Also Available

Steven Katz, Lisa Ain Dack, & John Malloy
Leverage the oppositional forces of top-down expectations and bottom-up experience to create an intelligent, responsive school.

Peter M. DeWitt
Centered on staff efficacy, these resources present discussion questions, vignettes, strategies, and action steps to improve school climate, leadership collaboration, and student growth.

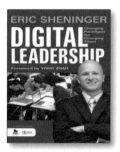

Eric Sheninger
Harness digital resources to create a new school culture, increase communication and student engagement, facilitate real-time professional growth, and access new opportunities for your school.

Russell J. Quaglia, Kristine Fox, Deborah Young, Michael J. Corso, & Lisa L. Lande
Listen to your school's voice to see how you can increase engagement, involvement, and academic motivation.

Michael Fullan, Joanne Quinn, & Joanne McEachen
Learn the right drivers to mobilize complex, coherent, whole-system change and transform learning for all students.

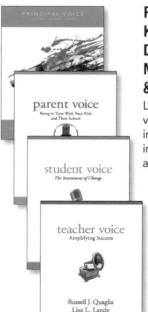

CORWIN
LEADERSHIP

A SAGE Publishing Company

Helping educators make the greatest impact

CORWIN HAS ONE MISSION: to enhance education through intentional professional learning.

We build long-term relationships with our authors, educators, clients, and associations who partner with us to develop and continuously improve the best evidence-based practices that establish and support lifelong learning.